—THE COMPLETE—
MAIGRET

THE COMPLETE
MAIGRET

**From Simenon's original novels to
Granada's much acclaimed TV series**

PETER HAINING

B🍃XTREE

G R A N A D A   T E L E V I S I O N

THE COMPLETE MAIGRET
by Peter Haining
Boxtree
1994

First published in Great Britain in 1994 by Boxtree Limited

10 9 8 7 6 5 4 3 2 1

Designed by Design 23
Typeset by SX Composing Ltd, Rayleigh, Essex
Printed and bound in Great Britain by Butler and Tanner Ltd for
Boxtree Limited
Broadwall House
21 Broadwall
London SE1 9PL

A CIP catalogue entry for this book is available from the British Library.

ISBN 1 85283 447 1

The author would like to thank the following for their help in supplying
photographs for this book: SIPA Press, Rex Features, Granada, Hulton
Deutsch, The Kobal Collection, the British Film Institute and *Punch* magazine.
All other illustrations are from the author's own collection.

Frontispiece: *Michael
Gambon – the latest
Maigret in the
Granada TV series.*

CONTENTS

"He would be, to some extent, a repairer of destinies, because he was capable of living the life of all men, of putting himself in the skins of all men."

MAIGRET'S FIRST CASE (1949)

INTRODUCTION

THIRTY YEARS AGO WHEN television was still in its black and white era, the French Commissaire, Jules Maigret, became a cult figure on BBC TV. In a three year period from just before Christmas 1960 to December 1963, the stolid, painstaking detective played by a Welsh actor named Rupert Davies became one of the most popular figures in the nation, the weekly stories on Monday evenings between 8.45 p.m. and the main evening News at 9.40 p.m. becoming compulsory viewing for millions of viewers throughout Britain. Not only did the series of fifty-one episodes make Davies a household name, but it proved the public taste for crime and mystery and became the forerunner of what is now arguably the most popular genre on the small screen: the detective story.

Thirty years later, Granada TV and Michael Gambon have turned Maigret into a cult figure all over again with a new series of adventures about the Chief Inspector which they began in 1992 and are continuing again this year. Nor is Gambon the only Maigret presently appearing on TV – in France since 1991, a series based on Georges Simenon's novels starring Bruno Cremer has been attracting ever-increasing audiences, while Holland, Russia

The current French Maigret, Bruno Cremer.

and Japan also have their own current Maigrets making regular appearances in annual 'Specials'.

The popularity of Maigret on the screen is, though, nothing really new. The Inspector actually made his debut on film in a 1932 movie, little more than a year after his creation, and then appeared on television when the medium was still in its infancy – in 1950 in America of all places! In total, Maigret has been portrayed by some twenty-one actors in a period of exactly sixty years, a record probably only exceeded by three other famous literary characters: Frankenstein, Dracula and that other great master of detection, Sherlock Holmes.

The legend continues – after the search for a new Maigret, the Daily Mail *breaks the story on 12 March 1991.*

SINGING DETECTIVE CROSSES THE CHANNEL

Acclaimed: Gambon as the Singing Detective

Strike a light! Gambon is new Maigret

Loved: Davies as Maigret

THE Singing Detective is changing his tune ... to that of the pipe-smoking French sleuth Maigret.

Michael Gambon is to star in a six-part series based on the Georges Simenon books. And there are high hopes that he will prove as popular as the classic TV Maigret of the early Sixties, Rupert Davies.

For those who still fondly remember the Davies programmes, beginning with the striking

| Daily Mail Reporter |

widow of his TV predecessor.

Top 'tec — Davies

Hunt for TV sleuth

TV BOSSES are hunting for a star to play French supersleuth Maigret in a blockbusting new series.

Granada TV want to make sure their seven-part series doesn't flop like last year's £3 million HTV production.

An insider revealed: "There have been a couple of big names ban-died around but no-one has been approached."

The original Maigret, played by Welshman Rupert Davies, was one of the most successful BBC shows of the Sixties.

Jean Richard, France's other famous contemporary Maigret.

The story of Simenon's creation of Maigret and the phenomenal success that has surrounded the indominatable Commissaire both in books and on the screen is one of the most remarkable to be found in either of these media. It is a story that I have set out to recount for the first time in the pages that follow – both in terms of the detective himself and the actors who have attempted to capture his unique characteristics and capabilities. It is a story that I have enjoyed investigating – and one that I am convinced will continue to exert its special fascination long into the twenty-first century, too.

PETER HAINING
January 1993

1:

THE MAN WHO WAS MAIGRET

COMMISSAIRE JULES MAIGRET of the Paris Police Judiciaire has been called the 'Sherlock Holmes of France' and in terms of worldwide fame and popularity he certainly deserves to be bracketed with Britain's most celebrated detective. Nor do the similarities end there – for like Sir Arthur Conan Doyle with Holmes, Maigret's creator Georges Simenon also tried to abandon him after writing eighteen cases, without fully appreciating his enormous popularity with the public who at once demanded his return. Both authors, too, have become very much overshadowed by the fame of their characters.

Georges Simenon at the time he was writing the Maigret *books.*

Cover of one of the first Maigret *novels,* Liberty Bar, *published in 1932.*

The final total of eighty-four novels and eighteen short stories about Maigret offers a fairly clear picture of *le patron* (as he is sometimes called) yet there are still enough enigmatic aspects to his character remaining to fascinate and intrigue each new generation of readers. That scholarly theses are now being written about Maigret almost as frequently as appreciative letters continue to be received by Simenon's publishers is a further

indication of the phenomenon he has become. For how else can a fictional character who has inspired numerous films and television series, been the subject of parodies and literary spoofs, had his likeness depicted on postage stamps and his culinary tastes duplicated by famous chefs, not to mention his name taken in vain in many a court case, be otherwise described?

The man himself is somehow unprepossessing yet unforgettable. Maigret is heavy set, 5 feet 11 inches tall, with broad shoulders and stolid features reflective of his bourgeois origin. Early in his career as an inspector he sported a thick moustache, and wore a well-cut suit, bowler hat and thick winter coat with a velvet collar, but as police fashions changed and he became a Commissaire so the moustache disappeared and the last two items of clothing were exchanged for a felt hat and mackintosh coat.

Essential for a detective, Maigret has exceptional eyesight and the ability to take a nap almost anywhere. He does, though, suffer from claustrophobia and when called upon to exert himself often becomes short of breath. He is a gourmet where food is concerned – listing among his favourite meals *fricandeau à l'oseille* and *pintadeau en croûte* – and loves a drink, preferring glasses of draught beer or a fine cognac, although he is quite happy to take virtually any type of alcohol.

The pipe that Maigret invariably keeps clamped between his teeth (as much a characteristic as his hands thrust into his coat pockets) is just one of fifteen in a rack in his office at the Judiciaire on the Quai des Orfèvres beside the Seine. His filing system there is notoriously disorganised, but he is well served by his three assistants, *le brave* Lucas (actually described in the novels as 'chubby' and able to pass himself off as Maigret's double), the family man, Janvier and the eager youngster, Lapointe. Despite his seniority, Maigret often joins his men in looking for clues,

though he will also send them off on inquiries while he blends into the environment of the crime that is being investigated.

The inspector does not drive, and prefers to use taxis and buses rather than the police cars which are available to him. Unlike most other detectives in fiction, he does not use ratiocination (the process of reasoning) when investigating a crime, but is an intuitive detective, putting himself into the scene of events and studying all those involved. It is his sheer presence that finally tends to expose the guilty person or overwhelm them into making a confession.

Though Maigret is often kept from his home for long periods when on an inquiry, he always looks forward to returning to his other life with Madame Maigret in their rather shabby but comfortable third floor apartment at 130, Boulevard Richard-Lenoir, not far from the Place de la Bastille. The couple's relationship is undemonstrative but undoubtedly extremely close, and at times they seem almost to function as one in their complete understanding of each other.

Madame Maigret's Christian name is Louise, but this is never used by her husband, nor does she ever refer to him as 'Jules'. A homely figure, she is a good cook, but over the years many a meal has gone to waste through her husband's failure to come home when involved on a case. The couple have no children, although there was a daughter who died in infancy, much to their sorrow.

When the Maigrets do have time to spend together they like walking or going to the cinema. Maigret occasionally reads the novels of Dumas, but *never* detective stories, and less frequently watches television, preferring westerns and grade-B movies to any other programmes. The couple appear to have only two close friends: the Pardons, with whom they dine twice a month. Maigret discusses psychiatry and the human character with the husband, a doctor.

An artist's impression of Maigret from the British magazine, Argosy.

Artist's impression of Maigret from Ici Paris.

The Maigret we meet in the first cases (published in the early 1930s) is about forty-five years of age. His earlier life history, which has also been outlined by Simenon, will be considered shortly in relation to his creator. In the last of the stories published four decades later, he has just about reached the mandatory retirement age of fifty-five. Throughout all these years, his greatest characteristic remains his infinite patience, while his compassion for his fellow human beings never waivers despite all the pain and suffering he sees them impose upon one another. His most single-minded pursuit is, beyond doubt, for justice.

Rarely, though, does Maigret express any views about himself, the one notable exception being in a later novel, *Maigret in Society* (1960) in which Simenon writes of the Commissaire: 'He did not take himself for a superman, did not consider himself infallible. On the contrary, it was with a certain humility that he began his investigations, including the simplest of them. He mistrusted evidence, hasty judgments. Patiently, he strove to understand, aware that the most apparent motives are not always the deepest ones.'

These, then, are the very human characteristics of Inspector Maigret which make him so appealing both as a detective and a man; an element almost completely missing in the machine-like Sherlock Holmes or Agatha Christie's effete Hercule Poirot. He is, quite simply, a greathearted human being. Giles Cooper, who adapted a number of his cases for television in the early 60s explains.

'What makes this rather large, and sometimes slow-moving detective so different? In the first place he is essentially a man of sympathy. With a brilliant insight into human nature, he is nevertheless often fallible. He possesses, as Simenon himself says, the approach to crime of a really first-class GP. His methods, too, are different from those of the usual police inspector. He much prefers calling on the person to be interviewed or interrogated to having him brought to his office. He goes, he looks, he smells, touches, senses, gets the feeling of the situation and the people he has to deal with. As a result he becomes inevitably involved in the action, suspense, danger, laughter – and he sees it all with the eyes of a great humanitarian.'

But even with all this information one is still forced to ask the question – *who* was he? For no such great literary figure has ever come wholly from the imagination. In this case, the answer seems to be simplicity itself: Maigret was none other than Georges Simenon himself.

According to one popular legend, the prototype of Maigret was supposed to have been an actual French detective, Marcel Guillaume, who died in 1963, aged ninety-one. Later that same year, however, when Simenon was asked about this story, he said he 'could not remember' where his inspiration had come from, but there were probably elements of his own father, Désiré in the detective. He elaborated further on this statement in a radio interview during the course of which he said: 'When I wanted to create a sympathetic person who understood everything, that is to say Maigret, I gave him without realising it certain of my father's characteristics.'

This is a view not altogether accepted by several of Simenon's biographers; in particular two of the most eminent, his long-time friend, Thomas Narcejac, and the English writer Fenton Bresler who also came to know him intimately. Narcejac, who published one of the earliest studies of the author's work, *The Art of Simenon* (1952) wrote:

'Maigret represents an ideal. He stands for every aspect of strength, including a certain plebeian roughness. But he does to an extent represent Simenon; the pipe, the hands in the pockets, the wandering gaze and that indefinable air of power and

An emotional Georges Simenon at the unveiling of the statue of Maigret by Pieter Dhondt at Delfzijl in September 1966.

refinement which show a man's calibre. In some of the details of his life and character Maigret tends to become completely free of his creator. He has a civil status, a profession, habits and eccentricities which give him a personal existence. But he sees and feels like Simenon. Hence a slight lack of unity and cohesion. He has a fictional truth as a civil servant and a human truth as a policeman.

He is alternately character and author.'

Writing thirty years after this in his *Mystery of Georges Simenon*, Bresler reached much the same conclusion: 'Maigret is not Simenon in any simple, straightforward way, but I believe that over more than four decades of close identification with the same character, with whom he had considerable similarities anyway (the intuitive way of working, the basic humanist philosophy, the pipe-smoking, the childless marriage – Simenon did not become a father until ten years after the first Maigret was written – the early flirtation with medicine as a possible career, etc), Simenon found that Maigret became in psychological terms, his alter-ego; an essential part of his life and of his personality.'

Bresler also adds later in his book: 'The nearest that Simenon has gone to acknowledging anything like what I believe to be the true relationship between himself and Maigret in the long discussions that I had with him was to call the detective *"mon brave Maigret"* and to say that, with the passage of years, he no longer knew who was Maigret and who was himself: one had merged so much into the other.'

When considering the facts of Simenon's own life in conjunction with the 'life' he devised for his character it is possible to find further evidence to support these writers' assertions.

Simenon, for example, was born in Liège, Belgium on 13th February 1903, the son of an insurance clerk, Désiré Simenon; while Maigret was 'born' in Saint-Fiacre in the Allier where his father, Evaride, was the bailiff of the estate. Both fathers had positions of dignity guaranteed to earn respect from their sons. Both author and character attended local Catholic schools, were choirboys, and briefly nurtured ambitions to become doctors. But while Maigret pursued this ambition at the University of Nantes until he was forced to leave because of the death of his father, Simenon took himself off to the 'university of life' in Paris where, after a brief spell as a private secretary, he found his métier as an author churning out hack novels for a local publisher.

Maigret also turned up in Paris, where he lived in a cheap hotel before gaining entry to the police force at the age of twenty-two. The young policeman began his working life patrolling the back streets and rubbing shoulders with petty criminals, gangsters and prostitutes, just as Simenon haunted the same streets looking for the low life and high adventures that would provide the material for his books. For both men, the insight into human nature that they gained during these years was to provide the basis on which they built their highly successful careers.

A third biographer, Stanley G. Eskin in his *Simenon: A Critical*

An illustration from the rare French booklet, Le Paris de Simenon, *which the author published in conjunction with artist Frederick Franck who illustrated several Maigret stories.*

Biography (1987) has further underlined the parallels between author and creator: 'The accumulation of personal details gives Maigret a certain density and they themselves are reinforced when they are related to Simenon's own experience and personality. Thus, as we have seen, young Maigret's arrival in Paris parallels Simenon's, as does his delight in bus platforms and sunny café terraces. They share childhood memories of choirboy duty, and Maigret once lived near Place des Vosges (as did Simenon). When Maigret furnishes his retirement home near Meung-sur-Loire, he had the same impulse as Simenon at La Richardiere to scour the countryside for antiques to furnish it. Maigret, like Simenon, considers himself a collector of men, as he

Interpretations of Maigret – contrasting French and English editions of the same title, both published in 1960. The Inspector on the Four Square edition bears a decided resemblance to Jean Gabin, the French screen Maigret of the time!

laconically answers the crooked art dealer in *Maigret et le Fantôme* when the latter tells him, ''You'll have trouble understanding me, you're not a collector . . .''.'

The remaining facts of Simenon's much-publicised life as a famous author living in France, America and Switzerland, his sexual prowess and claim to have slept with 10,000 women as well as the tragic suicide of his beloved daughter, have been well documented. With two new biographies imminent, they require no further discussion here. Appropriately, he signed off his career as a novelist with a book about the Commissaire, *Maigret et Monsieur Charles*, but was unhappy at the parting as he admitted in 1973: 'I feel full of remorse for having completely dropped Maigret after *Maigret and Monsieur Charles* – it is rather as if one has left a friend without shaking his hand.'

Simenon's own obituaries in September 1989 similarly regretted his passing. *The Times* declared: 'Simenon has been compared to Balzac, and he was made a member of the Légion d'Honneur, but he once said that he had a ''horror of Literature''. The plainer the words, he argued, the more universal the appeal. His main achievement was, by such plainness, to turn the simplest of *romans policiers* into a moving and memorable form of art.'

There is one more suggested influence on Simenon's work which I think should perhaps be mentioned: Sherlock Holmes himself. In most discussions about the creation of Maigret, the idea of Sherlock Homes lurking somewhere in the background has always received short shrift. But in fact, Simenon admitted that he had read the Sherlock Holmes cases when he was young, and actually set out to create a detective who was the absolute opposite to Conan Doyle's 'reasoning machine'. A policeman who intuitively understood how human beings ticked and as a result of this understood how and why both murderer and victim behaved as they did.

What there can be no argument about is that Simenon wrote the first story about Maigret, *Pietr-le-Lotton* (*The Strange Case of Peter the Lett*) in 1929 while he was on a sailing expedition on his new yacht. He had bought the *Ostrogoth* shortly beforehand with some of the money earned from his 'potboilers'. The vessel was moored in the little Dutch port of Delfzijl when the idea for a big, powerful policeman who solved crime by intuition came into his head.

'I did not see his face,' Simenon said years later. 'Just his massive presence. I still do not know what his face looks like. I only see the man and the presence.'

While it is true that Simenon had already written some crime stories amongst his hack work – and had actually used the name 'Maigret' for a policeman in one of them – it was at this moment that he had the first clear idea of the sort of man he was going to write about.

'You see, a detective is a kind of rope,' he explained, 'you follow him and he can go into people's houses and ask questions. I never worked out my plots in advance. In fact, I discovered the criminal's identity at precisely the same time as Maigret.'

Although the publisher, Artheme Fayard in Paris, to whom Simenon took his first Maigret story, expressed doubts about its potential, he agreed to publish it if the author would write several more so that they could be launched as a series. This the enthusiastic young man (he was then just twenty-six) agreed to do. Once the slim volumes began to reach the bookstalls, their appeal was immediate and their sales enormous. From that moment on, Simenon, who also quickly learned how to strike a good bargain with publishers over royalties, rapidly became a multi-millionaire. He could tell journalists without a trace of false modesty: 'Since I thought of Maigret, I have never been poor.'

Truer words have rarely been spoken. In 1972, Simenon was reckoned by UNESCO to be one of the most translated writers in the world and his books had been read by an estimated 500 million people. Of his titles, ranging from 'pulp' romances and westerns to the 'hard' novels (which, like Conan Doyle, he considered his best work) and the Maigret crime stories, it was said

Rupert Davies as Maigret with Ewen Solan as his faithful assistant Lucas in the 1960 BBC TV series.

Michael Gambon with (left to right) James Larkin as Laponite, Geoffrey Hutchings as Lucas and Jack Galloway as Janvier in *Granada's 1993 version.*

that approximately 220 had appeared under his own name, and at least the same number of novellas under seventeen different pseudonyms. Even the fact that in the autumn of that same year, 1972, Simenon announced that he would write no more fiction – and was true to his word until his death in September 1989 – did not result in any appreciable falling off in his annual sales. More than one authority has called him, with justification, the most prolific novelist the world has ever known.

The success of the Maigret novels and short stories has not been confined to the printed page, however. As this book will show, the detective was seized upon for the cinema screen almost as soon as he appeared and, in the fullness of time, has been adapted equally successfully for television. Although the vast sales of the Maigret novels have certainly established the inspector's fame with a worldwide audience of readers, his image is equally familiar to many other people who may never have read even one of the books. Millions of cinema-goers and television-watchers now 'know' Maigret – a fact entirely due to the actors who have

impersonated him during the past half century.

It is now, in fact, just sixty years since the first screen Maigret, Pierre Renoir, appeared as the inspector in *La Nuit du Carrefour*. In the light of the long history of Maigret in films and on TV, it seems entirely appropriate that this should have been the first story to reach the screen, for when translated into English, the title was changed to *Maigret at the Crossroads*. Since that date we have had an endless flow of actors; French, English, Italian, German, Dutch, American, even Russian and Japanese – all in their different ways endeavouring to capture the essence of this remarkable character on the screen.

Could there be a better moment, especially with the Granada series starring Michael Gambon now successfully established, to look back over sixty years of film and TV productions that have each, in their way, played a part in making the character? In the words of that doyen of crime writers, Julian Symons, Maigret is 'the archetypal fictional detective of the twentieth century'.

Welcome, then, to the world of Maigret on the screen . . .

2

MAIGRET IN THE CINEMA

THE MAKING OF THE first Maigret film was highlighted by a number of remarkable, even bizarre, events that could easily have come from the pages of one of Simenon's own novels. The story which began the tradition was *La Nuit du Carrefour* (*Maigret at the Cross-roads*) directed by Jean Renoir and starring his brother, Pierre, as the first screen Maigret.

The events which were to culminate in this earliest movie began in August 1931 when Simenon was still living on board his boat, the *Ostrogoth*, though it was now moored, semi-permanently, in the harbour of Ouistreham on the Baie de Seine. The author was particularly happy in this environment, sitting each

Jean Renoir, the great French film maker, and the first director to bring Maigret to the screen.

day on the deck, pounding out new Maigret stories for his eager readers and at night carousing with the local sailors and fishermen, often challenging them to tests of strength at arm wrestling.

Simenon was hunched over his typewriter, pipe in his mouth, on the morning a large Bugatti sped into the harbour and screeched to a halt alongside the *Ostrogoth*. When the dust had settled, the figure of Jean Renoir, younger son of the great impressionist painter, Auguste Renoir, and who was himself destined to become one of the most famous names in the French cinema, leaped up the gangplank to confront the startled author.

'At last, Simenon, I have found you!' Renoir is reported to have said. 'I wish to buy the film rights to *La Nuit du Carrefour*. Your book will make a splendid movie.'

As the novel – the sixth Maigret in Simenon's contract with Fayard – had appeared just two months earlier, the author's amazement at his visitor's words can be imagined. Taking Simenon's silence to indicate that the rights were free, Renoir promptly offered him the sum of 50,000 francs. Simenon said later he could only nod his head in agreement. Those few words and the writer's instant agreement probably amounted to the quickest and simplest deal ever made for the screen rights to a major literary character.

Since that summer day, both men have recounted their own versions of what was a landmark moment in the history of Maigret . . .

Jean Renoir had been in the business of making films since 1924 when he had produced, scripted and even acted in his first film, *Une Vie Sans Joie*. Thereafter he had produced a number of artistically brilliant but financially unsuccessful silent movies, most starring his father's former model, Catherine Hessling, a beautiful redhead whom he had married. During this period, Renoir had also undertaken a number of commercial directing assignments in order to raise money for his own projects, in which he was striving to develop the sense of visual realism which would later become his hallmark. The coming of 'the talkies' presented him with a new challenge, and one of the first films he decided to produce with sound was an adaptation of *La Nuit du Carrefour*. Renoir has explained how this came about in his revealing autobiography, *My Life and My Films* (1974):

'After a period of involuntary unemployment, neither my first nor my last, I again yielded to the temptation to produce a film of my own. The money came to me from private sources, nothing to do with the film trade. The story was based on a wonderful novel by Simenon entitled *La Nuit du Carrefour*. Jacques Becker was production manager; my nephew, Claude Renoir, was assistant cameraman; the script girl was Mimi Champagne and Jo de Bretagne was in charge of sound. All friends, in short, with my older brother Pierre playing the leading part.'

Simenon, for his part, could not have been more delighted that Jean Renoir was to be the first man to bring Maigret to the screen.

'From my first days in Paris at the time of the *avant-garde* cinema, I had been one of Jean Renoir's greatest fans,' he said in *Intimate Memoirs* (1984). 'I knew his first wife, Catherine Hessling, who was so overwhelming in *The Little Matchgirl*, one of his first masterpieces. After he had bought the film rights to *Maigret at the Crossroads* we did the screen treatment together, in a rented villa at Cap d'Antibes, and I met his brother Pierre who was the first actor to play Maigret.'

As a result of this association, Simenon and Renoir became life-long friends, and the author was later to confess that he felt 'very honoured' that the film maker should have wanted to produce the Maigret story. 'I would have given him the rights free,' he admitted. 'He was for me like a brother.'

Pierre Renoir (1885-1952), the brother chosen to play Maigret, was an imposing character actor. At twenty-two, he had won the Premier Prix de Tragédie at the Paris Conservatoire. His early career had been spent almost entirely in the theatre – interrupted by the First World War in which he was injured – and *La Nuit du Carrefour* was to be his first venture into talking pictures. His resonant voice, world-weary features and dark, brooding eyes made him an ideal Maigret.

Simenon's dramatic story tells of the discovery of the body of an Antwerp diamond merchant in an unidentified car at a small garage at the crossroads of Trois-Veuves near d'Arpajon, and how Maigret is stymied in his investigations until he witnesses the shooting of the murdered man's widow. It offered Jean Renoir the perfect opportunity to use his skill at visual realism, as he explained:

(Opposite, above) *Pierre Renoir, the brother of Jean Renoir, and the first Inspector Maigret in* La Nuit du Carrefour *(1932).* (Opposite, below) *an uneasy alliance of suspects in the first Maigret film,* La Nuit du Carrefour.

'My aim was to convey by imagery the mystery of that starkly mysterious tale, and I meant to subordinate the plot to the atmosphere. Simenon's book wonderfully evoked the dreariness of that crossroads situated fifty kilometres from Paris. I do not believe there can be a more depressing place anywhere on earth. The small cluster of houses, lost in a sea of mist, rain and mud are magnificently described in the novel.'

Renoir decided to film the picture entirely on location at the actual setting of the story. When he discovered that one of the houses at the crossroads was empty, he hired it and set up his

headquarters there. What followed proved to be an experience that no one involved would ever forget.

'A good many of the team slept on the floor of the living-room,' he said later, 'We had our meals there. When the darkness was as mysterious as we wished, we aroused the sleepers and went to work. Within fifty kilometres of Paris we led the life of explorers of a lost land. Marcel Lucien, the cameraman, achieved some remarkable fog effects, and the actors, both amateur and professional, were so influenced by that sinister crossroads that they became part of the background. They enacted mystery in a way they could never have done in the comfort of a studio. *La Nuit du Carrefour* remains a completely absurd experiment that I cannot think of without nostalgia. In these days, when everything about films is so well organised, one cannot work in that kind of way. Nevertheless, in the matter of mystery, the result exceeded our expectations.'

The film, though, suffered problems during the making. Renoir had constant worries over the finances which several times delayed shooting, and his marriage to Catherine Hessling was also on the verge of breakdown, causing him an emotional crisis. One result of these strains was that several key scenes were missing when the final version was being prepared for release in 1932.

The mystery as to what exactly happened to these scenes – amounting, it is said, to two reels of film – has been much debated. According to one story the reels were lost somehow between the location and Renoir's studio in Paris; while another source has suggested that they were deliberately not shot by Renoir in order to create 'a dramatic disjunction corresponding to an aesthetic discontinuity'. As in many such cases, the truth is actually far simpler, and the mystery was finally resolved by Simenon himself shortly after Renoir's death in 1979.

'Even now I don't want to speak ill of him,' Simenon said, 'and his death upset me greatly. But when they were making that film, Jean was in the middle of separating from his first wife, Catherine Hessling, the actress. He was very depressed and in the morning he started to drink and drink and drink, and he was nearly drunk most of the day. He directed the scenes that he shot very well but he forgot some, and when they saw the whole thing it was too late because they were already engaged in another film somewhere else.'

Not surprisingly, according to Renoir, when the picture was shown to a selected audience it was found 'pretty well incomprehensible, even to its author'. In a desperate attempt to salvage the movie, the producer offered Simenon a fee of 50,000 francs – the same as he had been paid for the film rights – to appear before the cameras and film a series of inserts to be placed in *La Nuit du Carrefour* at key moments to explain the plot.

Tempted though he was by the money, Simenon could not bring himself to do it. 'Fifty thousand francs was a lot of money in those days,' he said, 'but I still refused. I had no desire to ridicule myself even for 50,000 francs!'

Despite its failings and the fact that it sank without trace at the French box office, this film of what is one of Simenon's closest approaches to the traditional detective novel, has become a cult Renoir picture. It is frequently shown to appreciative audiences at cinema clubs around the world. The famous French director, Jean-Luc Godard, is among the most vocal admirers of this extraordinary picture, declaring it 'the only great French detective film ever made.'

A little of Simenon's disappointment was tempered by Pierre Renoir's outstanding performance as Maigret. Indeed, later in his life and after a dozen other actors had taken on the role, he was to describe the actor as 'the best Maigret ever – because he understood that Maigret was basically a government functionary.'

Whatever its shortcomings, *La Nuit du Carrefour* went some way towards showing the cinematic potential of Maigret. Before the end of 1932, a second producer had offered the public another story of the inspector. Like its predecessor, *Le Chien Jaune* (literally 'The Yellow Dog', but known in England as *A Face For A Clue*) was purchased by an independent film maker, Jean Tarride, who also cast a relative in the leading role. In this case, however, the man was his father, Abel Tarride (1881-1948), a veteran of the stage who in both age and looks was scarcely like Maigret. This film, though, was to prove a commercial success.

According to Simenon, the ink on his contract with Renoir was hardly dry when Jean Tarride, also infused with enthusiasm for Maigret, arrived in Ouistreham to purchase the film rights to *Le Chien Jaune*. The tale of *le patron's* investigations in the little Breton port of Concarneau, which is being terrorised by an unknown criminal, has been described as reminiscent of a story from the American 'hardboiled' school of detective fiction. Certainly both the novel and the film introduced a variety of sordid and colourful characters.

Tarride initially hired Simenon to work on the screenplay, but unfortunately the two men did not see eye-to-eye on a number of plot variations and within a short time they had parted company. Simenon's interest in the making of the second Maigret can be said to have ended there and then.

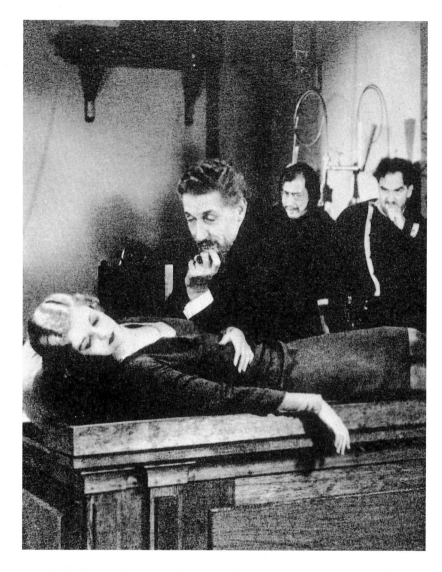

A rare still from the second Maigret film, Le Chien Jaune, *made in 1932 and starring Abel Tarride.*

A Face For A Clue was shot mostly in a Paris studio, with Abel Tarride giving a performance that has been described as 'far too over-ripe for the essentially humanistic and unflurried detective'. Yet the French public liked the picture. For a time Jean Tarride tried to capitalise on the American aspects of the story – a bootleg-liquor operation being worked across the Atlantic – in order to get a dubbed version distributed in the USA, but without any success.

The making of the third Maigret film also ran into a number of problems, and was to complete Simenon's disillusionment with the film industry. The sale of the rights to *La Tête d'un Homme* (known in England as *A Battle of Nerves*), however, ensured Simenon's financial stability, as he wrote in his Memoirs:

'From the first Maigrets on, it was mainly the movies that acted as good fairies. The sales to Jean Renoir and Jean Tarride were to be followed by the sale of *La Tête d'un Homme*, and then so many other novels, which paid for my Chrysler, a stay in the most beautiful villa at Cap d'Antibes, the setting up of La Richardiere, and the purchase of three horses, and finally a trotter and sulky. Sometimes I went two or three years without selling my movie rights – or, more precisely, leasing them, for one language only, for a period of seven, eight or at most ten years.'

The man who was ultimately to make *A Battle of Nerves* a memorable picture was the director, Julian Duvivier, but this was not until the project had very nearly foundered. Fenton Bresler describes what happened: 'In April 1932, it was announced in *Vu*, a leading French cinema magazine that, "M. Georges Simenon, the well-known author of numerous detective stories, will himself direct *La Tête d'un Homme*, one of his latest novels, of which the principal role will be taken by the great artiste, M. Valery Inkinijoff." In the end, *La Tête d'un Homme* did appear on French screens, being premiered in Paris the following February, but it was a totally different film from that undertaken by Simenon. Funds ran out before they even started shooting and the project was taken over by another producer with Julian Duvivier, an experienced director, replacing Simenon behind the camera, and the great Jewish actor, Harry Baur, coming in for M. Inkinijoff as the third film Maigret.'

Thereafter, says Bresler, Simenon lost all interest in the project. He did not interfere as Duvivier re-wrote the script and changed several of the characters in the story of Radek, a man blocked from realising his ambitions legally, becoming instead a criminal mastermind involved with some unsavoury American millionaires. Nor did he make any comment when a singer named Damia, who had nothing whatsoever to do with the plot, was introduced into the film to sing a couple of numbers. This, apparently, was a common practice in the French film industry at the time: to garner publicity for the picture by releasing a record from it.

According to Stanley Eskin, Simenon was so soured from this experience 'that he rarely had anything more to do with film versions of his works, and embodied his jaundiced view of the movie industry in several novels, such as *Le Voleur de Maigret*.' This said, *La Tête d'un Homme* has its admirers and like Renoir's *Nuit du Carrefour* is occasionally reshown today with admiring notices for Baur's performance.

Harry Baur (1880-1943), the third screen Maigret, has been

described as 'a lion of the French cinema throughout the thirties'. During his movie career which effectively began with the coming of sound, he played many leading roles including Shylock, Jean Valjean in *Les Misérables*, the composer in *The Life and Loves of Beethoven* and the mad Russian monk, Rasputin, all of them earning him a place as one of the dominant actors of the European cinema during that era.

Baur made his acting debut on the stage in 1906 when he played a number of roles in the famous Grand Guignol Theatre which helped him to develop a versatility for every kind of part from comedy to high drama. At 6 foot tall, weighing 200 pounds and with heavy, dark features, Baur closely matched the Maigret of Simenon's stories.

Harry Baur who gave one of the cinema's most admired performances as Maigret in La Tête d'un Homme *(1933).*

As its English title suggests, *A Battle of Nerves* is a tale of police detection as Maigret attempts to track down a murderer who is seen right at the outset at the scene of his crime. A review published in 1960 when the film was reshown as part of a season of 'undeservedly neglected French classics', summarised the plot neatly:

'*La Tête d'un Homme* is primarily a tale of police detection, but Duvivier's predilection for the "special case" in human experience may well have drawn him to Simenon's novel for the sake of its psychological motivation. Though the action is not hampered by study of motives; murder, nonetheless, is no mere matter of financial advantage. Radek, the murderer, is a doomed and desperate creature, with a morbid lust for life and for revenge on it. Motives are sufficiently sketched in to achieve the "vraisemblance" to touch off the spark of dramatic conflict and give body to the characters – to Inspector Maigret, with his relentless yet compassionate pursuit of justice, to the coldly acquisitive promoter of the crime and his calculating mistress, and to the half-witted scapegoat, blundering into the trap set for him and waiting in a dumb agony of bewilderment for release.'

Duvivier enjoyed directing Baur in the film, for as he later wrote: 'Baur often surprised me. He had unexpected intonations, absolutely original expressions. In *Poil de Carotte* the role of Lepic brought him a deserved success. But as Commissioner Maigret he really excelled himself.

'Baur and his pipe were truly Maigret. When he was before the cameras he became Simenon's character. He was always Harry Baur, though, amiable, hearty and sincere – but he was also, in a striking way, the character of the story.'

Reviewers, too, enjoyed the movie when it was released in 1932, *Le Figaro* speaking for the majority when it declared: 'The suspense is born of dramatic encounters like that of the scapegoat with the murderer across the body of the victim, of the Inspector's inquisition of the half-wit and his confrontation of the murderer – heightened here by the contained, implacable gaze of Harry Baur's Maigret.'

Fate had a grim end in store for Baur, although the precise details are somewhat clouded in mystery. According to the first version based on German sources, Baur was arrested and shot by the Gestapo in 1942 for posing as an Aryan.

A report in the *London Evening News* of 13th October 1942 quoting the German Press Exchange and datelined Zurich, has this story: 'Berlin film circles say the French film actor Harry Baur has been executed for having counterfeit proofs of Aryan identity, "thus persuading the German film industry to give him a prominent part in a film costing nearly two million marks which it is now necessary to destroy".'

According to the second version of Baur's death, in 1942 his Jewish wife was arrested in Paris by the Germans who shortly afterwards seized him in Berlin and charged him with being an Allied agent. Later the actor was sent back to a French prison, tortured by the Gestapo who, unable to extract a confession from him, released him in April 1943. Several days after his release, it was said, he died 'mysteriously'.

A Reuters' report that I have discovered in the pages of *The Daily Telegraph* of 29th September 1944 seems to confirm this later version: '"I prefer dying upright to living on my knees," Harry Baur the French film star, told his Gestapo torturers in Cherche Midi Prison, Paris, where he was held for over a year. His death soon after his release was reported by Reuters yesterday.'

Such are the facts about Baur's death, and the mystery surrounding it is surely one that Maigret himself would have enjoyed investigating. Interestingly, too, a biographer said of him: 'His intense concentration on his work and his passion for accuracy even in small details is reminiscent of Charles Laughton.'

That was to prove an apt and prophetic comparison, for in 1949 the self-same Charles Laughton was to pull on Maigret's hat, take out his pipe, and play the Inspector in a re-make of *A Battle of Nerves* retitled *The Man on the Eiffel Tower*: of which more later.

Because of Simenon's disillusionment with the film industry, it was to be almost a decade before Maigret appeared on the screen again. As the author himself said after his experience with *La Tête d'un Homme* 'I made a decision, to which I remained faithful for more than five years, of not selling the film rights in any of my works to anyone, whatever the increasingly large amounts I was offered.'

The fact that Simenon was now a wealthy man with royalties pouring in not only from his French publisher, but also those who had translated him abroad, made such a stand possible. And, indeed, it was not until the outbreak of the Second World War when France was occupied by the Germans, that he relented to the blandishments of film makers – a fact which was to cause him some embarrassment.

'I wasn't stopped from making my films in the war,' he said some years later. 'They continued to make Maigrets. I asked myself why actors shouldn't be allowed to go on making their living because there was a war. So I let my films be made. But some people found it – how shall I say? – in bad taste.'

The French actor, Albert Prejean, who was the first star to play Maigret three times on the screen during World War Two.

Such misgivings apart, the next film featuring Maigret was also something of a milestone in that it introduced the first of the 'series' inspectors in the person of Albert Prejean (1893-1979), who was to repeat the role three times between 1943 and 1945. A former boxer, racing cyclist, night club singer-acrobat and much decorated First World War fighter pilot, probably no actor before or since, brought such a diversity of talents to the role – not to mention skill and endurance!

In the light of his early chequered career, it is perhaps not surprising that Prejean entered the film business as a stunt man in a number of French historical pictures including *The Three Musketeers* (1921) and Raymond Bernard's *Miracle of the Wolves* (1924). An elegant young man, very thin and handsome, it was only a matter of time before he was offered a proper acting role in *Paris Qui Dort* (1924) which also marked the directorial debut of the famous, Rene Clair. The two men made several more pictures together including *Le Chapeau de Paille d'Italie* (*The Italian Straw Hat*) in 1927 which helped make Prejean's name, and two years later Clair's first sound film, *Sous les Toits de Paris*, in which he portrayed a Parisian street singer.

Prejean had played a detective inspector before making his trio of Maigret films. This was in Pierre Chenel's *L'Alibi* in which that master of villainy, Erich von Stroheim, appeared as the suspect he was pursuing on a murder charge.

The first of Prejean's Maigret roles was in *Picpus* (*To Any Heights*) made in 1943 about the *clochard*, Mascouvin, who has been enlisted to play the role of a deceased husband so that the widow can continue to collect the proceeds of an inheritance. The Inspector's task in getting to the bottom of the plot is not helped by a series of bizarre events and some even stranger people whom he encounters during his inquiries.

Picpus was directed by Roland Pottier, an admirer of Simenon's stories, who was also responsible for casting Prejean as Maigret despite some initial opposition from the backers. These reservations proved ill-founded, for the star carried off the part with quiet determination and no little style. This was no easy thing to do, as Prejean himself has explained in his autobiography, *The Sky and the Stars* (1956), as Paris in 1943 was the target of frequent Allied bombing raids:

'We were in the studios when the skies and roofs of Paris were split open by air raids,' he wrote in the staccato style that also typified his acting. 'The moment the first wails of the siren were heard you could see Maigret, his superintendents, inspectors and sergeants capering along at full gallop, elbows well tucked in, towards the nearest shelter. We dived several yards below ground, murderers, detectives, informers and false witnesses, corpses and pathologists, and stood squashed one against the other while the bombs burst over our heads.

'The all-clear sounded and we would gingerly pop our noses out of the doors. Back we would go to our former positions on the set. Back to the cameras and Maigret's wise deductions. Another wail of siren; a second stampede; a further flight of pseudo corpses who didn't want to become real ones! Temporarily suspended were the wise deductions!'

To a man who had earned a chestful of medals in the air, ducking falling bombs on the ground was not something to disturb his natural calm and *Picpus* emerged from these difficult conditions as a well-crafted and engrossing movie. It was successful with audiences, too, providing the kind of escapist fare that lacked any trace of political implications which might bring the Gestapo tramping into a cinema to stop the film and close down the place.

This success also prompted thoughts of a follow up, and Prejean was quickly signed up to make *Cecile est Morte* (*Maigret and the Spinster*) which was shot in the summer of 1944. Unfortunately, Pottier was committed to another project, but the adept Maurice Tournier, who had worked in Hollywood for a dozen years and then returned to Paris some years previously, was available. His track record, including the classic crime story, *The Mystery of the Yellow Room* (1914) and *L'Homme Mystérieux* (1933) made him an ideal substitute.

In this story, Maigret investigates the murder of an avaricious, crippled old woman, set against the background of a neighbourhood just outside Paris teeming with a variety of strong characters. The original novel was very much a psychological tale of repressed passions, and although the film took a number of liberties with Simenon's original, it was well served by Tournier's suspenseful direction and another compelling performance by its star. (In 1955, another French actor, Maurice Manson, starred in a re-make of *Cecile est Morte* entitled *Maigret Mene L'Enquête*, directed by Stany Cordier, but this proved both an artistic and financial failure of which very little record survives today.)

The last of Prejean's trio of Maigret pictures was *Les Caves du Majestic* (*Maigret and the Hotel Majestic*) which was filmed shortly after the Liberation in 1945. For this picture, he was also reunited with Pottier as his director.

For the first time, a considerable amount of the film was shot on location in the Avenue des Champs-Elysees where the Hotel Majestic stands. Now there was no danger from falling bombs,

Maurice Manson who made an undistinguished appearance as the Inspector in Maigret Mène L'Enguête *(1955) also appeared with Brigitte Bardot in* A Woman Like Satan, *directed by Julian Duviver who had produced and directed the third Maigret picture,* La Tête d'un Homme.

only over-eager Parisians who crowded around while each scene was being shot. It took all Pottier's legendary patience to complete the picture on time and within budget.

The tale of a rich American widow discovered strangled in the posh Hotel Majestic and the finger of accusation pointed at the establishment's humble little coffee men, Prosper Donge, is what brings Maigret into a situation complicated by personal rivalries and jealousies among the staff. *Les Caves du Majestic* was the first Maigret film to have a short-lived release in America during a vogue for French films in the early fifties when it was shown with subtitles as *Death on the Champs Elysees*.

For cinema-going Parisians during the war years, Prejean had become 'the' Maigret and there are older people who still remember this versatile and likeable man today. When he died in November 1979, *Variety* magazine described him as 'one of the most popular leading men in the French cinema between the wars who portrayed Inspector Maigret three times on the screen.'

If Prejean can be credited with introducing Maigret to American cinema audiences for the first time, it was to be a British-born actor who would make him well-known, not only in

the United States and England, but wherever else the picture was shown. The man's name was Charles Laughton (1899-1962).

Laughton, the son of a Yorkshire hotel proprietor, abandoned the catering trade for acting and was at first sight an unusual choice to play Maigret. Certainly, he had prior experience of portraying detectives, having been the first to appear as Agatha Christie's hero, Hercule Poirot, on the London stage in 1928 in *Alibi* (based on *The Murder of Roger Ackroyd*), as well as playing the other side of the coin as a gangster, Tony Pirelli, in Edgar Wallace's production, *On The Spot* (1931) which ran for fourteen months. But his robust and boisterous screen style seemed the antithesis of Maigret's characteristics.

Yet Laughton was a performer with a wide range of styles and perhaps sensed a fresh challenge when he was approached by the American producer-director Irving Allen in 1949 to star in a remake of the Harry Baur story, *La Tête d'un Homme*, now to be called *The Man on the Eiffel Tower*, and in which Maigret would conduct a cat-and-mouse game in the streets of Paris to find the murderer of an elderly woman recluse. He was also, by his own admission, hard up for money.

Charles Laughton, the first Englishman to play Maigret in The Man on the Eiffel Tower, *with co-star Burgess Meredith.*

Allen, who was born in Poland but educated in America, was a crime buff and had become increasingly convinced that Maigret could be as successful on the cinema screen as he was in Simenon's books. He negotiated a deal with the author and then set about hand-picking his players. Apart from Laughton, he also recruited Robert Hutton, Franchot Tone and his wife Jean Wallace, plus the great character actor Burgess Meredith, who was a friend of Laughton and may well have been influential in getting him to join the cast. It was not, though, to prove a happy experience for either man, as Charles Higham has described in his 'intimate biography', *Charles Laughton* (1976):

'Once he had accepted the contract, Charles threw himself into preparing the role of Maigret with his customary intensity, driving over to Western Costumes in Hollywood and selecting a bowler hat and dark suit to convey the temperament and meticulous nature of Simenon's famous detective. Untidy himself, preferring to wear shapeless trousers held around his waist by ancient frayed neckties, Charles as always proved able to sink himself into a character, and the Maigretesque suit he took to Paris was brushed and spotlessly clean. However, knowing that Maigret was apt to be absent-minded, he always made sure that the suit was badly pressed and a little baggy. He read and re-read the Simenon stories to work himself into the right mood.'

Here, indeed, was a professional actor going about his job in a very professional manner: especially in his decision to wear an outfit similar to that described in the early Simenon novels. But there was a noticeable lack of professionalism awaiting Laughton at the Villancourt Studios where the picture was to be made on a three-month shooting schedule, according to Higham:

'After three days, Charles found it impossible to work with Irving Allen as director. He insisted that Burgess Meredith take over. Allen was furious, but when Charles threatened to return to England, he was forced to give in, staying on as producer only. There were many problems during the shooting. The Ansco-Colour process was weird, creating bizarre distortions. Autumn rain delayed the shooting for days. Irving Allen, resenting Charles, quarrelled with him constantly. Local electricity shortages caused a series of power failures, plunging the set into darkness.'

With hindsight, the disasters accompanying this, the first Maigret to be filmed in colour, seem very similar to those that had plagued Jean Renoir's first black and white production, *La Nuit du Carrefour*. A fact that may well not have been lost on both Meredith and Tone who had worked with Renoir and knew about his troubles as a film maker. (Tone later attempted to film Renoir's biography, but died before the project could be completed.)

Work on the picture was finally completed, however, but not without some further dramas while filming a complicated series of chases across Paris and a final sequence on the Eiffel Tower in which Tone took his life in his hands by walking on some narrow girders about 800 feet from the ground without a safety net.

According to Higham – who, as Laughton's biographer, might be guilty of a little bias – the only good sequence in the picture was one actually directed by the star and featuring his friend, Burgess Meredith.

'Charles' directorial opening was masterly,' Higham wrote, 'an eccentric, gnome-like knife-grinder, typical of Meredith's well-known gallery of oddities, enters a house in Paris and stumbles over the blood-drenched corpses of a rich American widow and her maid. The slow, loping knife-grinder's walk, the stealthy climb upstairs to burgle a room, the shocking touch of a corpse, bloodstained hands spread out as the horrified man races down the stairs – the sequence had a macabre power that looked forward to Charles' major directorial achievement, *The Night of the Hunter*, five years later.'

According to Higham, *The Man on the Eiffel Tower* was crude and overemphatic and was doomed to both critical and popular failure. But this is not strictly correct. The film was certainly only modestly reviewed, but it more than made its money back and has been reshown at least twice in cinemas as well as several times on television. Simenon, who was living in Arizona when the picture was released, saw it himself and said he liked it – although he felt that the bowler-hatted Laughton neither looked nor spoke quite like his idea of Maigret.

Whatever the merits of this movie, it certainly caught the interest of a substantial American audience – a fact born out by the decision of two popular American weekly television shows to introduce Maigret to their viewers, first in 1950, and then again in 1952. These productions, which mark the debut of the inspector on the small screen, are, of course, of special significance and will be dealt with in some detail in the next section about Maigret on television.

In the meantime, back in France, Maigret was to be portrayed by two outstanding actors whose performances would set standards that have still not been surpassed, in the cinema at least . . .

The first of these stars was Michel Simon (1895-1975), a hulking, heavy-featured actor who made two Maigret pictures, *Le Témoignage de l'Enfant de Choeur* (*Elusive Witness*) in 1952 and ten years later starred in a joint French-Italian version of *Le Bateau d'Emile* (never translated). Born François Simon in Switzerland, the son of a Geneva sausage maker, Simon had, considering his ungainly size, a remarkable ability at playing comic or dramatic characters with a mixture of power and deftness.

Michel Simon gave a memorable performance as Maigret in Elusive Witness *(1952).*

There was also about him something of Albert Prejean, his predecessor in the Maigret role, for he, too, had pursued a number of careers – including those of boxer, photographer and music hall clown-acrobat – before going onto the stage in 1918. And like the current incumbent of the role, Michael Gambon, Simon was a big, shambling figure, with a distinctive deep voice and an admiration of animals, especially the ape family. Indeed, his home on the outskirts of Paris was famous for its menagerie of animals, including dogs, birds, cats and five monkeys. When one of these monkeys named Catherine who had been his constant companion for twenty years died, he was inconsolable. Simon even refused a number of film roles that involved cruelty to animals.

Like Gambon, too, Simon was described as a man with 'a homely face and teddy bear body' who possessed a wicked sense of humour and earned the respect and admiration of his fellow professionals for his dedication to his art. His connection with the Maigret legend extends still further for he came to public notice in two films directed by Jean Renoir, *La Chienne* (1931) and *Bondu Sauvée des Eaux* (1932), and established his *basso profondo* talent in Julian Duvivier's *La Fin du Jour* (1939). Francois Truffaut who also directed him in a later picture said of his ability to bring ordinary and unglamorous characters to life: 'When Michel Simon plays a part, we penetrate the core of the human heart.'

This was an ability which Simon used to good effect in both his performances as Maigret. *Elusive Witness* was actually one of three stories in an anthology of detective tales released under the generic title, *Brelan d'As (Brelan the Ace)* – the other two stories being *Mort dans l'Ascenseur* by S. A. Steenan, and a Lemmy Cauton adventure, *J'ai le Coeur Tendre* by the English crime writer, Peter Cheyney. The Maigret episode was based on a short story of the same title in which Simenon drew on his own childhood memories as a choirboy to recount the inspector's pursuit of the killer of a young chorister.

A contemporary French report of the making of the film in Paris describes Simon's performance as Maigret in these words: 'The manner in which this prodigious actor puts himself into a role is always remarkable – his stature is such that he has to enlarge his roles to fit him and by so doing gives them life. As Maigret, he smokes his pipe, a short briar, with which he shrouds himself in smoke while he thinks and makes his deductions. He is taking the evidence of a chorister in this "crime without a body" about which his lieutenant, Rignault, does not appear to be concerned. The three of them are there in the banal atmosphere of a police office, Maigret, his assistant, and the choirboy, Claude

Fourcade, a youth of ten who has already made as many films as he has years, and who is quietly waiting his opportunity for really entering this medium of entertainment.

'Henry Verneuil – whose *Table aux Caves* marked a brilliant directorial debut – directs with a good humour which nevertheless misses nothing. But the presence of Michel Simon on a set immediately gives it that something . . . and it is not just his ability to tell a funny story. He does everything with an amusing good grace and charm. He does nothing that would rouse the curiosity of visitors or disturb the work of the technicians. He gives way obligingly and is never aggressive. He has a sharp and mordant wit that is not noticeable in his characterisations. For many people he is soon going to be *the* Commissaire Maigret, that very popular character in French detective fiction.'

Reviews of *Brelan d'As* singled out the Maigret episode and Michel Simon's performance as the best part of the film, but it was not until 1962 that he was seen in the role again. In the interim, his career had very nearly been destroyed in 1957 by a nightmare experience which occurred while he was working on a film entitled *Un Certain Monsieur Jo*. For the part Simon was asked to dye his moustache black and a chemical in the dye poisoned his skin and penetrated his nervous system, paralysing part of his face and body. Both his vision and his voice were impaired for almost two years before he was well enough to act again.

This had not been Simon's first brush with suffering. During the First World War he had contracted tuberculosis and spent several years in a sanatorium. Meanwhile, during the German occupation of France, his home was taken over by the Gestapo who persecuted him for allegedly being Jewish until he was able to obtain papers proving his Catholic background. After the war, he was also unfairly accused of being a Nazi collaborator because he had made a number of films with the overt approval of the Germans. When his life was threatened by members of the Résistance, he was for a time forced to travel everywhere with two bodyguards whenever he was working.

These experiences gave him a special insight into the background of the Maigret story, *Le Bateau d'Emile*, based on another short story, which was directed by Denys de La Patelliere and co-starred Pierre Brasseur and Annie Giradot. The story of a man with a mysterious past who is being persecuted and has taken to the river to try and escape his fate was one that Simon could relate to well. Once again he brought the Maigret of Simenon's story to life in a performance that was both measured and commanding whenever he was on screen.

For Brasseur, who played the persecuted Emile, it was his second encounter with a Maigret, for he had actually studied acting with Harry Baur and appeared with him in a couple of movies. A fine character actor who could mix wit and irony, Brasseur made an ideal foil for Simon and the film undoubtedly benefitted from their partnership. Brasseur later appeared in a number of other detective stories including the critically-acclaimed *Crime Does Not Pay* (1962).

Simon had one more association with the Maigret story before his death in 1975. This occurred in 1960 when he appeared on a Swiss television documentary about Simenon and his work, *Simenon, Abre à Romans*, produced by Jean-Francois Hauduroy. Extracts from his two films were shown, and Simon also played a scene from a non-Maigret novel, *Le Président*, as the venerable lawyer, Augustin, reviewing some of his past triumphs at the bar. Once again viewers were given a hint of how much Simon might have contributed to the Maigret legend if he had played the inspector more than twice.

Jean Gabin (1904-1976), the charismatic French film star and most recent cinema Maigret, appeared in three movies about the Commissaire between 1958 and 1963, and as a result is the best-known screen actor to have played the part. Like Michel Simon – with whom he appeared in *Quai des Brumes* (*Port of Shadows*, 1938) – he owed his rise to fame through appearing in films by Jean Renoir and Julian Duvivier. His roles as strong, silent and often doomed human beings have deservedly earned the accolade of 'the tragic hero of the contemporary cinema' given to him by the film critic, Andre Bazin.

Gabin's success was also helped in no small degree by his association with the work of Simenon. Apart from his three Maigret films, he also appeared in another seven screen adaptations of the author's works: *La Marie du Port* (1950), *La Vérité sur Bébé Donge* (1951), *Le Sang à la Tête* (1956), *En Cas de Malheur* (1958), *Le Baron de l'Ecluse* (1959), *Le Président* (1961) and *Le Chat* (1970).

In all performances as Maigret, Gabin used his unmistakable deep voice and slight movements of the eyes or mouth to suggest a whole range of emotions – the kind of suggestive techniques a good policeman would use to cajole evidence from a witness or a confession from a murderer. These qualities plus his almost square head set on a solid body and his 'stumping' way of walking which hinted at tremendous energy, provided him with all the necessary elements of Maigret's character. Of the actor himself, Renoir once wrote, 'Gabin could express the most violent emotion with a mere quiver of his impassive face.'

Gabin was the son of musical hall artistes, but though he had a good singing voice, he had no ambition to work in the theatre. It was only at nineteen, after several years as a labourer, that he allowed himself to be persuaded by his father to join the *Folies Bergère* as a bit-part player. Following several years on the stage, latterly as Mistinguette's leading man, he allowed himself to be talked into the film medium.

In the movies, Gabin soon demonstrated that he could play a wide variety of roles, but was especially good at anti-heroes such as the laconic criminal in *La Bandera* (1935) and the gangster in *Pepe le Moko* (1937). He could be at his most effective playing a gangster leader dominating the forces of both good and evil – not to mention the screen – by his sheer presence. At the outbreak of the Second World War, Gabin decided to move to Hollywood and although he again found himself in the company of Renoir and Duvivier, who had also sought exile, it proved to be neither a happy nor particularly successful period of his career.

(Opposite) *the great Jean Gabin – for many French fans the greatest Maigret.* (Below) *Gabin filming in the French backstreets which Maigret knew so intimately.*

*Maigret (Jean Gabin)
talking to two suspects
in* Maigret Tend Un
Piège *(1957): (Below)
with Olivier Hussenot
and (Opposite) Annie
Giradot.*

Back in France, he began his association with the works of
Simenon in 1950 in *Le Marie du Port*, and then in 1958 appeared on
the right side of the law for the first time as a lawyer in Simenon's
En Cas de Malheur in which his co-star was the young Brigitte
Bardot. It was an ideal prelude to his debut in the role of Maigret
in *Maigret Tend un Piège* which he filmed later that year under the
direction of Jean Delannoy.

Delannoy, an actor before he took to directing, had become
well-known for a string of popular thrillers such as *Savage Triangle*
(1951), *The Moment of Truth* (1952) and *Obsession* (1954), and had
been keen to adapt a Maigret novel for the screen for several
years. When *Maigret Tend un Piège* (*Maigret Sets a Trap*) was

published in 1955, he knew he had found an ideal subject in this story of a series of brutal murders of attractive young girls in Montmartre. The killer turns out to be a psychotic painter with a mother complex who not only eludes the inspector but also taunts him. Delannoy worked on the script himself and decided that Gabin would be the ideal man to play the dogged inspector on the trail of the vicious killer.

Gabin's portrayal of Maigret was different to those of his predecessors, with less reliance on the props such as the pipe and hat and more on his ability to portray the emotions running through his mind. As one critic wrote: 'In all Gabin's portrayals it was a quality of absolute integrity and emotional truth which com-

pelled the attention and respect of audiences. He may not have looked like the Maigret of popular imagination, but he was certainly the Maigret of heart and spirit.'

Co-starring with Gabin in the film – which was later released in Britain and America as *Inspector Maigret* – was Annie Giradot who, of course, had appeared with his predecessor, Michel Simon. She played Yvonne Moncin the wife of the morbid painter at the centre of the killings, Marcel Moncin. Interviewed during the course of filming, the sensual, award-winning actress was diplomatic about her preference as Maigret:

'*Le Commissaire* is a man of such fascination to the general public that it does not matter if a dozen different actors play him, there will always be something new to discover,' she said. 'Both Michel Simon and Jean Gabin have approached him in their own ways and they are equally valid. As men they are so different: Michel is so outgoing and has such humour, while Jean is more of a private person.

'But Jean is like Maigret in that he loves cooking! Sometimes between shots he would talk about his favourite meals and give tips to the actors and members of the film crew. Then he would return to the cameras and be right back in the mood of the part again. Formidable!'

The general public also shared Giradot's enthusiasm for the new Maigret, and less than a year later Delannoy adapted another of the early novels, *L'Affaire Saint-Fiacre* (*Maigret Keeps a Rendez-vous*) published in 1933. The story was of particular interest to admirers of the Maigret saga for it was set in the inspector's 'birthplace' where his father had been the bailiff and he himself had been a choirboy. It concerned the murder of the Comtesse de Saint-Fiacre while she was attending mass and involved the machinations of a disaffected nobleman culminating, according to one critic: 'in a lurid climax straight out of the Gothic tradition'.

The part of this sophisticated man-about-town was played by Michel Auclair, the German-born former stage star who was known for the subtlety of his acting, and later worked in a number of prestigious European and American movies, including *The Day of the Jackal* in 1973. Auclair told an interviewer during the course of filming that he was an avid reader of crime novels, especially those of Simenon, and claimed that he rarely failed to spot the murderer before reaching the denouement.

The second Gabin/Maigret proved less successful at the box office, but a third was shot in 1963, based on a more recent novel, *Maigret, Lognon et les Gangsters*, which had been published in 1952. The story set against the background of Quartier de l'Etoile might

well have been written for Gabin in his gangster era – though here he was the detective out to catch a pair of American gangsters named Tony Ciccro and Charlie Cinaglia accused of murdering another American killer nicknamed 'Sloppy Joe' Mascarelli. Attempting to assist Maigret on this case was the memorable Inspector Lognon, the accident prone and melancholic policeman who would very much like to be part of *le patron's* team. The mysterious female who crosses Maigret's path at every turn was played by Françoise Fabian, later to become internationally famous when she starred in Luis Buñuel's *Belle de Jour* (1967).

Stylistically, the picture differed considerably from its predecessors because the director, Gilles Grangier, was a film maker who worked quickly and put action above characterisation. He, too, had been an actor before turning to directing and, as a great admirer of Gabin, grabbed at this opportunity to work with one of his heroes. (He was, in fact, to direct more Gabin 'quickies' in later years.)

Released as *Maigret Voit Rouge* (*Maigret Sees Red*), the third Gabin film was to prove his finale as the inspector. Like the first two, however, it was shown in Britain and America; although in

(Above and overleaf) *The inscrutable Maigret homes in on the murderer in the 1959 movie,* Maigret et L'Affaire Saint-Fiacre.

Britain, where people were just reaching the end of the three-year series of Maigret stories on television featuring Rupert Davies, many now found his interpretation of the French police-man not entirely to their taste.

In fact, the movie was to be the last Maigret film made specifi-

cally for the cinema. The Commissaire had now found a whole new TV audience on both sides of the Atlantic. The facts about these adaptations, the actors who appeared in them, and how they helped develop this new element of the Maigret tradition which continues today will be the subject of the next section . . .

3

THE INSPECTOR ON TELEVISION

WHENEVER MAIGRET ON television is discussed it is a widely-held fallacy that it was the British actor, Rupert Davies, who first brought the inspector to the small screen in a hugely popular and long running series of fifty-two episodes for the BBC which was shown in the early sixties. In fact, Davies had already been preceded in the role in America by two other television stars, and in Britain by a distinguished actor who appeared in a pilot episode for the BBC series, but then decided against continuing in the role when the decision to make the programme was approved.

These three 'forgotten' inspectors are an important element in both the start and the development of the television Maigret and have not previously been studied in any book about Simenon's work. My research in both London and New York has uncovered some interesting facts about the actors themselves as well as the adaptations in which they appeared – not the least of these being that it was American television, and not British or even French TV, that first introduced Maigret to the viewing public.

Television in America at the start of the fifties was a far cry from the TV we know today. Public transmissions had only begun in the country in 1941 – almost five years behind Britain, where the BBC had started the world's first public television service in November 1936. Amcrican TV shows were in black and white and virtually all were broadcast 'live'. For this reason, no copies of the first two made-for-television Maigret dramas are believed to exist today.

Productions then were very much subject to unforseen technical hitches that could black out the screen at a crucial moment or perhaps cause the amusing sight in a murder story of a 'corpse' suddenly getting up and walking away when the actor believed he or she was off camera. But by all accounts no such problems bedeviled either of the two versions of the Maigret short story, *Stan the Killer*, about the identity of the leader of a murderous Polish gang exposed by Maigret, which were transmitted in 1950 and 1952 from the CBS Studios in the heart of New York City.

Most of the weekly TV series then had sponsors and often a host to introduce the stories to viewers. Such was the case with the dramatic anthology show, *The Trap*, hosted by Joseph DeSantis, which provided Maigret with his television debut on 20 May 1950. It was, for its time, an auspicious debut — on a top rated show put out in the peak viewing hours of 9.00 to 10.00 p.m. *Stan the Killer* was, in fact, only its fourth presentation and starred two leading television actors, Herbert Berghof and E. C. Marshall, both of whom would become well-known in the movie industry.

All the stories presented on *The Trap* were described as being concerned with people who had got themselves into situations over which they had no control. 'Fate would be the determination of their future,' a press release about the show stated, 'of whether or not they survived the perilous predicament into which they had got themselves trapped.'

The Maigret short story in which the inspector lies in wait to arrest the members of Stan the Killer's gang, who have been robbing farms and brutally killing their occupants before hiding up in Paris, fitted neatly into this concept — especially with its startling denouement. It also suited the restrictions of television in the early fifties in that the events occur almost entirely in the Hotel Beausejour or in the street directly in front of it, the Rue Saint-Antoine. Consequently, a street scene, the cramped reception area of the hotel and one of its starkly furnished rooms were the only sets the production required — plus a little stock footage of familiar Paris scenes to set the atmosphere.

The man who created Maigret for this production was Herbert Berghof (1909-1990), an Austrian-born actor who later became one of the most influential American drama teachers. Born the son of a station master, he studied acting in Vienna and worked with a number of classical drama companies throughout Europe until the Nazis overran Austria. When most of his family were either killed or imprisoned, he was smuggled to England and from there went to New York where he continued to act in the theatre and in the embryonic television industry. (In the fifties, New York was the centre of the TV industry, and it was only when an increasing number of programmes went over to pre-filming that the emphasis switched to the West Coast and Hollywood.)

As a man who had experienced injustice at first hand, Berghof was a suitable actor to cast in the parts of either policemen or gangsters. He had, in fact, played a number of such roles before appearing as Inspector Maigret in *Stan the Killer*. A description of his appearance in the broadcast indicates that he played Maigret as a cigarette-smoking, rather shabbily dressed figure: in some respects a forerunner of Peter Falk's Colombo. His mastery of European languages did, however, enable him to invest the character with a strong French accent.

Television's first Maigret, Herbert Berghof, who appeared in the 'live' adaptation of the short story 'Stan The Killer' on American CBS TV in May 1950.

The role was just one of many that Berghof took at this time, all having to be learned, rehearsed and acted before the cameras in the space of a week. Aside from television, he also appeared in several feature films in which his dark, brooding good looks were instantly recognisable, including the spy drama *Five Fingers* (1952), *Fraulein* (1958) and *Cleopatra* (1962).

Stan the Killer, in fact, retained no special memories for Berghof, although his part in it was recalled by E. G. Marshall, the veteran actor who made a speciality of playing men of the law and won two Emmys for his portrayal of the righteous lawyer in the TV series, *The Defenders*. Marshall appeared in the role of Michael Ozep, a former Polish Army officer who insists on helping Maigret in his efforts to catch the murderous gang.

'Herb was one of those guys who could slip on a part along with the suit he was given by the costume department,' he said recently. 'He was good at playing cops because he had a strong face and a way of narrowing his eyes that seemed to see right into a person's soul. He was a very good actor, and he was an even better teacher.'

Just how good a teacher Berghof was may be judged by the fact that among the talents he nurtured in his New York studios were Anne Bancroft, Liza Minnelli, Al Pacino, Steve McQueen, Bette Midler, Jason Robards and Robert de Niro. When he died on 26 November 1990, his obituaries were full of tributes to his skill as an instructor. Sadly, not one mentioned the role he had played in being the first actor to bring Maigret to the television screen.

Studio One, the series which presented the second hour-long version of *Stan the Killer* at 10.00 a.m. on 9 September 1952, had for years been one of CBS Radio's most popular drama programmes and was then equally successfully transferred to TV in November 1948. Thereafter, it presented some of the most visually exciting stories in the early days of the small screen. The producer, Worthington Miner, drew his material widely, everything from the classics to crime stories, and with an hour-long show and a major sponsor in Westinghouse Electric was able to recruit top quality actors. Charlton Heston, Robert Keith and Yul Brynner were just three young talents who made their early reputations on the series.

Miner wrote the script of *Stan the Killer* himself and also cast the heavy-featured and brooding actor Eli Wallach (1915-) as Maigret. The other major role of Michael Ozep was played by Romney Brent, the Mexican-born leading man whose career was to include starring roles as Don Juan and Zorro.

Wallach, born just a stone's throw from the CBS studios in

(Opposite) *Illustration from* TV Guide, *20 May 1950, promoting the transmission of 'Stan The Killer'.*

Brooklyn, had made his acting debut at fifteen and after military service in the Second World War, had come to prominence as one of the leading exponents of Lee Strasberg's 'Method' school of acting. He demonstrated the range of his talents in several Broadway productions and then in television, before heading for Hollywood and his stunning debut as the unscrupulous seducer in Elia Kazan's box office smash-hit, *Baby Doll*.

In fact, Wallach's role as Maigret was to be one of his last wholly on the side of the law, for thereafter he played a succession of mean heavies of dubious morals. On TV he impersonated the inspector as a slick, Fedora-wearing officer, blunt almost to the point of rudeness and obviously intent on catching Stan's gang by any means at his disposal. He was seen carrying a gun on several occasions and – very un-Maigret-like – interrogated friends and enemies alike by sticking his face close to theirs and glowering very threateningly.

Like Berghof, Wallach remembers his time working for television as generally extremely demanding and occasionally monotonous, though he has a certain affection for *Studio One* because of its innovative camera techniques and for allowing actors far more freedom of expression than most series of the time.

'A lot of TV drama was in a strait-jacket then,' he has said. 'The sponsors were more interested in getting their message across

Stock film footage of Paris was used in both American TV productions of the Maigret *story 'Stan The Killer' to intersperse the 'live' studio action.*

Eli Wallach, who later made a career playing law-breakers on the screen, actually appeared as the second TV Maigret in another version of 'Stan The Killer', transmitted in the CBS series, Studio One, *on 20 September 1952.*

than having a good production, in case it might stop the viewers from thinking what they were supposed to buy the next time they went to the store. *Studio One* favoured dramas from Europe and they had some really good script writers like Rod Serling and Gore Vidal. Not to mention some up-and-coming young directors such as George Roy Hill, Frank Schaffner and Sidney Lumet. I did a couple of detective stories for them, including a Maigret story which must have been one of the first on TV.'

Not quite the first, but perhaps the better of the two because of Miner's higher production standards, more exciting camera techniques and five sets which included a street scene big enough to allow traffic to pass outside the Hotel Beausejour. What remains a curious fact is that since that date no other American TV company has attempted their own version of a Maigret story – despite the fact that Simenon was then living in the country (he remained in America for almost a decade from 1946 to 1955), his books sold by the million year in and year out, and the influence of *le patron* on the entire detective story genre could hardly be underestimated.

It was to be the BBC, in fact, who would next seize on Maigret's potential for TV and launch their ground-breaking series which truly earned the accolade 'memorable'.

Although it is now well known that Simenon himself negotiated all film and television deals for his work, there is no such record for *Stan the Killer* – which probably explains why the two transmissions are so little known today. (It seems probable to me, however, that, as the story was first translated into English in 1949 for the American journal Ellery Queen's *Mystery Magazine*, the sale was made through the magazine's publisher.) When the BBC approached Simenon a few years later about buying the rights to a number of Maigret stories for a TV series, there is plenty of evidence to draw upon.

Writing in his *Memoirs*, Simenon says that he was first approached by the BBC in 1958 when a representative told him the Corporation was interested in acquiring the rights to fifty-two stories. But, apparently on the advice of his friend Somerset Maugham, he decided to reject the offer. The BBC, however, persisted, and the following year sent another representative to France and found the author in a more amenable mood. He drove a hard bargain, but soon a little piece of history was in the making.

The rights which Simenon granted the BBC were for English-speaking countries only – with the exception of America – and the prints were to be made available to other countries with whom he might wish to make separate contracts for subtitled or dubbed versions. The license was to be for twelve years and would allow each TV station one screening and a repeat. The completion of this contract was signed in London and followed by a press conference, as Simenon has described:

'At the press conference the BBC man announces the news and I in turn tell how happy I am about it. But I am rather surprised to read in the papers the next day, particularly in the French papers which were represented at the press reception, big bold headlines such as the ever-recurring CONTRACT OF THE CENTURY, and, in France, A SIGNATURE WORTH A BILLION FRANCS. (At the exchange rate of the period, of course. Because the contract called for payment in pounds sterling, I never did work out whether that figure was correct or not.)

'There was, however, one clause in the contract that I did not read carefully, and which I was to become aware of only a dozen years later. It provided that, at the expiration of the contract, all prints and negatives were to be destroyed in the presence of a bailiff, so that today there is no trace left of those fifty-two Maigrets.'

But such thoughts were far from the author's mind in the first euphoria of completing this major deal, for, as he added: 'The films were to be shot in France, in the very locales where my novels took place, and the Welsh actor cast as Maigret, Rupert Davies, would turn out to be perhaps the best inspector of them all. He would become famous overnight, so famous that a future Prime Minister took him along on one of his election campaigns.'

True in essential details as Simenon's recollection is, it completely overlooks the fact that Rupert Davies was not the first choice as Maigret and nor did he appear in the first of the BBC's productions. This distinction belongs to an actor named Basil Sydney (1894-1968) who, though older, was strikingly similar to Davies in both looks and manner.

Apart from the fact that Sydney had the same heavy set features and stolid figure as Maigret, it was curiously appropriate that he should have been the BBC's first choice for the inspector. He had worked with the earlier film Maigret, Charles Laughton, in *Salome* in 1953, and like several of his predecessors on the large screen had played every kind of role from a gangster to a king.

Born in St. Osyth, Essex, the son of a provincial theatre manager, Sydney was destined for the stage and found his particular niche playing all manner of classical roles from 'heavies', such as Claudius, to Romeo and even young Marlow in *She Stoops To Conquer*. His work for the stage frequently took him to New York, and from time to time he augmented his career by employing his considerable gifts as a stage designer. In the post-war years he also made several films, including a co-starring role with Sir

Laurence Olivier in *Hamlet* (1948), as well as appearing in a number of television dramas.

Sydney was picked for the role of Maigret by Campbell Logan, a BBC producer who had long admired the Simenon novels. It had been decided to test the British public's interest in the detective by featuring him in a seventy-five minute production on the prestigious, prime-time programme, *Saturday Night Theatre*, just before Christmas on 6 December 1959. The pilot story chosen was *Maigret and the Lost Life* (1954) and the dramatisation was commissioned from one of the leading TV writers of the period, Giles Cooper.

Sydney, though, was totally surprised when he was invited to play Maigret: 'In all my years on the stage and in films I had never played a detective before,' he said at the time. 'In fact I don't like mystery stories, so many of them seem to cheat on the reader. I'm afraid I have never read any of Simenon's books either, and the only detective I know anything about is Sherlock Holmes.

'But as soon as I read the script I could see Maigret was nothing like Sherlock Holmes – he seemed to be a much more human policeman, more compassionate and a lot less like a machine. I decided I would play him as kind, painstaking and as human as possible, not like the usual brash and cliché-ridden detectives who turn up on television nowadays.'

The actor utilised a turned down hat and muffler, plus the traditional pipe, in conjunction with his own stocky, sturdy figure to give what most viewers later agreed was a reasonable impression of the Maigret of the books.

Logan also lined up a strong cast to support his star including Philip Guard as Lucas, Andre Van Gyseghem as Janvier and Henry Oscar as Lognon, while Anne Blake played Madame Maigret. Patrick Troughton (later to be the BBC's extrovert second Doctor Who) appeared as Albert the barman, who is very much at the centre of the story of Maigret and Lognon's patient search for the killer of a quiet, lonely young girl whose body has been found in a street near the Place Pigalle.

For the black and white transmission, the producer shot a number of scenes on location in Montmartre and staged the interiors at the BBC Studios. Wisely, he avoided an undue 'frenchification' of the production – instructing the actors not to try and indicate that they were supposed to be French by speaking broken English – then one of the perennial problems when doing foreign stories on television.

The BBC trumpeted their scoop in bringing Maigret to the screen 'for the first time' (sic) with a special feature in the *Radio Times*. 'Along with Sherlock Holmes and Hercule Poirot, Georges

Simenon's Commissioner Maigret must rank as one of the best known and best loved detectives in fiction,' the journal stated. 'The secret of his popularity, apart from the success with which his efforts are invariably rewarded, must surely lie in his compassion and his understanding. For Maigret is by no means the cold-blooded sleuth, piling up evidence in a clinically efficient manner before making his arrest. His first interest is in the people he is dealing with, whether they are the victims or the perpetrators of a crime.'

Although the production attracted the usual substantial audience for *Saturday Night Theatre*, the newspaper critics were mixed in their opinions. James Thomas of the *Daily Express*, while praising the attempt to bring to TV 'the Sherlock Holmes of France' found that Maigret, 'never really came to life – and if you have not the time to establish the atmosphere of the inspector's Paris, and the strange warmth of his personality, it is better to leave him alone'.

Dilys Powell, *The Sunday Times*' doyenne among reviewers, did not agree. Writing that she found it strange that Maigret had only just reached the TV screen, she went on: 'Giles Cooper dramatised *Maigret and the Lost Life* most adroitly, and Basil Sydney was inspirationally cast as Simenon's wry, humane, philosophical sleuth. Not perhaps a lifelike portrait of any policeman you ever knew: a Gallic Charlesworth with better digestion and a more benign sense of humour. I am assuming that we shall see much more of Maigret, for this was the gentle art of the whodunit on a much sleeker level than that to which we are accustomed.'

Maurice Richardson in the *Observer* also felt that although the BBC had tried very hard with their first Maigret 'something was not quite right'. He felt the choice of a post-war story as against one from the early period was a mistake to launch the character and 'the contrast between the film sequences and the live studio part was very sharp and the tempo, despite some agile and imaginative editing and camera work, was dismally slow and the acting was patchy'. Richardson added, 'Basil Sydney's Maigret was not really in the role, nowhere near gruff enough, too much like an ex-RAF Group Captain who keeps a pub in the Thames valley. They will all have to try again, perhaps not quite so hard.'

Peter Black of the *Daily Mail* continued this theme, but much more positively: 'The idea of adapting Simenon's Commissioner Maigret has been staring television in the face for years,' he said. 'Last night he arrived . . . and Basil Sydney made him an immensely entertaining and original detective. He established at once the possibilities of a whole new field of adult detection drama for television to explore. We must have more Simenon-Sydney, and that right soon.'

In hindsight, Powell's assumption and Black's foresight can be seen as uncannily accurate, although another actor was to fulfil the promise embodied in that first transmission. As for the proto-type English Maigret, in 1962, Sydney, then sixty-seven years old, was plunged into a real-life drama when he was attacked by three thugs in Hampstead, and although he fought off his attackers he had to be rushed to hospital for medical attention. Thereafter, he rarely worked again and died on 10 January 1968.

The memory of his appearance as Maigret also seemed to die with him, too, because only a single obituary notice made any mention of this fact – and by then as far as the general public was concerned there was only one Commissioner . . . Rupert Davies.

For a great many people, what remains the most memorable element of the BBC's Maigret – apart from Davies himself – was the opening title sequence and the haunting music that accompanied it. The rasp of a match against a wall, the flickering light on a watchful face beneath a familiar felt hat and the sound of a Paris street accordion became an unforgettable memory for millions of television viewers. It still rings through the minds of many of them today, over thirty years later.

Despite the reservations in some quarters about the Christmas production of *Maigret and the Lost Life*, the decision to proceed with a first series of thirteen stories was made by the BBC Drama Department. It would be the biggest project the Corporation had attempted to that date and was to be made with a level of documentary realism that would hopefully appeal not only to British viewers but also to an international audience as well. The BBC decided to appoint a new producer for the series, the experienced Andrew Osborn, and to look for a new Maigret as Sydney was unwilling to be committed to a programme which would demand all of his time for at least a year.

Osborn, as a former actor himself, knew how vitally important good scripts would be for the success of the series and had no hesitation in signing up Giles Cooper, who had done such a good job on the pilot, to be the Script Editor. Osborn spoke later of the problems of transcribing Maigret from the printed page to the television screen.

'The difficulty of dramatising any novel for television lies in the necessity for condensation,' he said. 'This problem is heightened, so far as Simenon's Maigret is concerned, because he lays emphasis not on action but on character and atmosphere. These are intangible qualities which the novelist can lay hold of and develop at length. Simenon has a genius for taking his reader into the minds of his characters. Somehow these intangible things must be captured and translated into pictures on the screen. The stories are often of great complexity. Simplification must therefore be applied, and, in so far as is possible, the story given a straightforward dramatic line.

'We were conscious that there are many Simenon fans who have built up over the years a clear picture of Maigret and the world in which he moves. We therefore wanted to be as faithful as possible to his original work. However, the limitations which condensation imposes upon us – time and the necessity of a strong dramatic form – often force us to take liberties. Minor situations and characters which may give great colour and atmosphere in the book can only be touched upon in the play.

'Those passages in the book which deal with the drama of the story have to be condensed into some visual form which moves our story forward and yet contrives to retain the essence of what may be very long passages in the book. Many characters and incidents must be sifted and shed. Lucas and Madame Maigret, for example, do not appear in many of the novels, but they are such interesting characters that licence was taken to introduce them into the plays.

Television's first famous Maigret, Rupert Davies, in the BBC series which ran from 1960 to 1963.

Murder in Montmartre
with Rupert Davies as
MAIGRET
at 8.45

MAIGRET
A Crime for Christmas
AT 9.40

The Maigret *symbol which became inextricably linked with the outstandingly successful BBC TV series.*

'Often one character in the play must take on the functions of many in the book. Also it may be desirable to translate into action those things which characters in the book merely talk about. Large and complicated scenes must often be avoided because they are beyond the scope of the television series. We have done our best to create atmosphere by authentic "sets" and short scenes filmed in the actual location mentioned by Simenon in his books.'

Osborn obviously had a clear vision of how he wanted to put Maigret on the small screen. Next, he needed the right actor to bring the inspector to life, and at the same time, to satisfy Simenon with his choice, as the author had asked for the right of approval.

The British acting profession in the early sixties was full of good character actors, but Osborn wanted someone who was not too well known or associated with any particular role and who had the stolid but compassionate look of Simenon's detective. In order to find such a man he combed the Who's Who of the acting profession and began to draw up a list of possibles for the part. Among the names on that list was Rupert Davies, with whom Osborn remembered working when he had been an actor himself.

The two men had appeared together in an episode of an ill-fated series, *Sailor of Fortune*, which had run for twenty-six hour-long episodes in the mid-fifties. Ill-fated because, for a drama pro-gramme much of which was supposed to take place at sea, it had been severely hampered by its studio-bound sets. The pro-gramme's Canadian-born hero, Lorne Greene, had afterwards exchanged his captain's hat for a stetson and become a star as Ben Cartwright in the Western series, *Bonanza*. Davies, his second in command, was, though, still looking for his big break in television when Osborn decided to call him in for an audition.

That audition and Davies' subsequent meeting with Simenon was not only to change his life but also to establish the tradition of Maigret on television which has continued to this day.

Davies, born in Wales in 1916, had no particular interest in act-ing when he was a youngster, a fact confirmed by an old school friend who later recalled he was known as 'Sparrow' Davies. The Maigret-to-be was a quiet, pleasant boy, said his friend, and as a prefect he gave the impression of being rather soft though he cer-tainly was not. The school friend added: 'He showed no sign of wanting to be an actor at that time. But when I came back from years of working in Africa and found he had become a star in *Maigret* I wrote to him. He invited me to meet him again and he was charming and quite unaffected.'

In fact, this charming and unaffected man had come into the acting profession via a most unlikely route during the Second World War. Serving as a regular in the Naval Fleet Air Arm, he had been shot down off the Dutch coast in August 1940 while an observer on a mine-laying flight. Thereupon he was hauled off to a German Prisoner of War Camp and spent five long, weary years, where his only distraction was to discover a talent for acting.

'I started by learning to play the drums in the camp band,' he said in an interview given when Maigret was launched on televi-sion. 'Then I took up acting to pass the time. I ended up produc-ing, directing and playing everything from Macbeth to Carmen Miranda!

'On my return to England on VE-Day, I still hadn't really thought seriously about acting as a career, but I was asked to appear in an all-ex-POW revue in aid of the Red Cross and it was then that the "bug" got me. So I left the Navy and started to look for work – but the only job I got in the first three months was the part of a diplomat in a documentary film about Smoke Abate-ment.'

It was an amusing situation for a pipe-smoking actor to find himself in, but times got better when he obtained regular work with the Company of Four where the great thespian Emlyn Williams encouraged him. This was followed by some parts in repertory and the Young Vic – including tours of South Africa and America – before he landed on the BBC's doorstep. Thereafter he did over 100 radio and TV programmes – ranging from *Mrs. Dale's Diary* to *Monitor* – as well as some West End parts and a few small roles in films.

The offer from Osborn to play Maigret was one that immediately appealed to Davies. He had already read some of Simenon's novels but realised the author would not be an easy man to convince he was the right person for the role.

'Simenon had lived with the character of Maigret for so long and developed him so brilliantly that he regarded him as a real person he knew intimately,' Davies recalled later. 'He had seen other actors play the inspector and I don't think he believed anyone had got him quite right.'

So in May 1960, Davies and Osborn flew from London to Lausanne to meet Simenon. It was a meeting about which both were nervous: if the actor was rejected it would mean the producer would have to begin his search all over again, while Davies' hopes for a full year of employment would be dashed at the first hurdle. Not surprisingly, he remembered their meeting in Switzerland very vividly.

'When we met Simenon he talked a lot about a variety of subjects before he got around to Maigret. I'm afraid that during most of that early conversation I fiddled with my pipe, looked for matches and ashtrays, and finally got down on all fours to fix the author's wobbling desk.

'Then, suddenly, I realised that he had stopped talking. Of course, he is also an inveterate pipe smoker, always has one in his mouth, and there are dozens of them hanging in rows in his home. He saw what I was doing, in particular the way I was fiddling with my pipe, and just exclaimed, ''The search is over. Here *is* Maigret!'''

Both Osborn and Davies were naturally delighted – and relieved – at this verdict, and shortly afterwards returned to London to begin making the series. Later Davies was to cherish a copy of one of the Maigret novels which Simenon gave him inscribed with the words: 'At last I have found the perfect Maigret', and later still, a bottle of liqueur with a note: 'To the English Maigret from the French Maigret, Bravo!'.

Simenon also remembered this meeting. 'I got to know Rupert Davies very well,' he said some years later. 'He was a very nice man and he did his best to feel his way into the part. I remember him visiting me at Echandens before he began the series and asking me to explain how Maigret behaved with his pipe and all that.

(Opposite) *Maigret (Rupert Davies) with one of his assistants, Lapointe, played by Neville Jason.*

'One thing, though, was rather amusing. I remember him saying to me: "Madame Maigret, as soon as she hears Maigret's footsteps on the stairs coming home, opens the door to him. It's as if she felt he was coming and he never needs to use his key. But what does Maigret do when he sees her? Should he kiss her or what?" I got our young chamber maid to come over and smacked her on the bottom and Rupert Davies blushed! "That's what you must do," I said, and that's how I showed him. It was only an affectionate gesture, nothing sexual, but all the same you could see that he had some difficulty doing it. Yet, he really was very good in the part.'

It was not just finding a 'very good' Maigret that would make the BBC series successful, however. It needed some equally accomplished co-stars, and the versatile New Zealander, Ewen Solon, was signed to play the much-developed part of Sergeant Lucas, and the attractive Helen Shingler was offered the role of the inspector's soulmate, Madame Maigret. Osborn decided to use at least one guest star in each episode as well.

There was also the matter of a catchy signature tune and background music – which the versatile Ron Grainer provided – and a designer who could recreate the inspector's Paris in the BBC studios at Television Centre.

In Eileen Diss, the producer made another inspired choice, for she brilliantly created the pungent and realistic French atmosphere which distinguished each episode. Diss took painstaking care with every item on her sets – from authentic-looking furniture to typically Parisian coffee cups and Gaulois cigarettes. Maigret's office, with its pipe racks, Paris street maps on the walls and a framed picture of Madame Maigret on the desk was actually a faithful representation of a real Chief Inspector's office in the Palais de Justice – including the identical Paris view from the window!

Speaking about her work, Diss said, 'Every time I went to Paris for a location trip I would come back with a wonderful assortment of bric-a-brac – posters, ashtrays, cigarette packets, even door knobs. Although half of these things may never be in sharp focus on the screen, if during a close-up you see a terribly French doorknob behind someone's left ear, it does make just that extra difference.' (That attention to detail, or 'extra difference', later earned her a design award, while one of her best sets – for the story of *Poor Cecile* – was put on show in the Design Centre in the Haymarket, London.)

Location shooting in Paris was fitted in between a schedule which allowed ten days to rehearse and record each episode in Studio 3. Then on Monday, 31st October 1960, the first fifty-five-minute Maigret, '*Murder in Montmartre*' dramatised by Giles Cooper and directed by Andrew Osborn was ready for transmission in the prime spot at 8.45 p.m. preceding the evening's main news. The week's issue of the *Radio Times* carried a photograph of Rupert Davies as Maigret on the front cover and a two-page feature inside which declared:

'There are not many people today who have not at some time or other come across the work of Georges Simenon; or who, having made the discovery, have not yet heard of Inspector Maigret. The two are now virtually inseparable. For Simenon has, since the age of twenty-five, written sixty or seventy Maigret stories, each one of which has been a bestseller. His work has been translated into some twenty-five languages and today Maigret is as famous in France, and elsewhere, as any detective to emerge from the pages of fiction in the past fifty years.

'His success is not surprising. For the character of Maigret, the large, benign, shrewd, understanding, intolerant, ruthless, gentle and modest pipe-smoking detective is a man Simenon has come to know as intimately as himself and with whom he himself can be closely identified.'

The *Radio Times* added further: 'The impact which Maigret has made in France has been tremendous, and has been largely responsible for a change in public opinion towards the French police. Until his appearance the police, in fiction at any rate, were presented with little sympathy and understanding. Maigret has done much to change all this and to present them in a truer light.

'And now Maigret comes to BBC Television with one of TV's most versatile and talented actors, Rupert Davies, as Maigret – a piece of casting which Simenon agreed could not be bettered. With this new series the BBC has also adopted a new principle – these Maigret productions are not films – although occasional film inserts are made as in any drama productions – but recordings of performances in the television studios.'

As a result of all this build up, Davies and his co-stars and the whole of the production team held their breath to see if the BBC's biggest gamble had paid off. Within minutes of the final credits rolling, Television Centre was receiving delighted phone calls from Maigret admirers all over the country, while the following morning's newspapers were quick to add their own accolades. Fred Cooke of *Reynolds News* spoke for the press *en masse* when he wrote: 'The BBC's crime series *Maigret* is as French as Gauloises and garlic . . . Rupert Davies has eased himself into the character until it fits him like a glove'; while Tony Gruner commented on the series from the professional's viewpoint in *Kinematograph*

"Monday—Maigret, Tuesday—Emergency Ward 10, Wednesday—Coronation Street, Thursday—Bootsie and Snudge. Friday—Dr. Kildare, Saturday . . ."

At the height of its popularity, BBC's Maigret *series made newspaper headlines and inspired cartoons such as this one from* Punch, *19 December 1962.*

Weekly: 'The acting quality has produced a standard that is far and above anything seen on British television.'

Within a month, the Maigret series was essential viewing for over ten million viewers every Monday night. 'Already, after only a few weeks, Inspector Maigret has become a topic of Tuesday morning conversation among millions of people,' the *Daily Telegraph* reported. 'Together with "Tonight", "This Is Your Life", "Panorama", and Maigret, the BBC is currently providing nearly three hours of entertainment which for variety, interest and quality would take some matching on any television network in the world.'

The overnight success of the series also dramatically changed Davies' life. 'Apart from the money, I now find I don't have to explain who I am as often as I used to,' he told one journalist. 'People stop me to talk about Maigret.'

Taking a holiday in Devon after finishing the first series, he was stopped so often by holidaymakers that he began to appreciate how a hunted criminal might feel. 'The maddening thing is,' he commented, 'that on the few occasions when I *would* like to be recognised, because it could be useful – like getting a table in a busy restaurant or cashing a cheque – it always turns out that the person I want to impress doesn't watch TV.'

There were two quite different reactions from viewers that had particularly amused him, he said. Leaving Television Centre one afternoon after filming he was approached by two small boys waving pieces of paper. As he walked away after signing his name, he heard one of the youngsters complain bitterly to the other: 'Hey, look at this – I thought you said he was Maigret.'

He also got a laugh from a remark made by his charlady. After the first episode she said, 'I'm disappointed. I thought you were going to be different. All those things you do on television you do at home!'

In fact, within a comparatively short space of time the actor was having to remind himself that he was Rupert Davies, actor – as more and more people came to see him as Maigret. Indeed, while he was filming outside the Palais de Justice in Paris, a police inspector walking by commiserated with him on the interference he was having to put up with in the series from the ubiquitous magistrate, Comeliau, his *bête noire*.

'I know what it's like,' the real inspector told the somewhat taken-aback actor, 'I have just the same trouble myself.'

Shortly afterwards, when Davies returned to London, he was stopped by a QC who invited him to the Law Courts, 'to see the British way of doing things'.

Just as the fictional sleuth Sherlock Holmes receives letters for help and advice from all over the world – handled by a secretary working for the Abbey National Building Society which occupies the premises which include 221b Baker Street – so Davies soon found himself getting mail at Television Centre addressed to Inspector Maigret.

Cartoonist Ronald Searle who later went to live in France, drew this appreciation of Simenon and his creation while the BBC series Maigret *was running in 1962.*

'They ask for advice, help, and gifts of pipes, pouches and tobacco,' he told another reporter in November 1961. 'People must think I chew up two pipes an episode although I've only got through one since the series started. I'm often asked to send a few pipes to be auctioned for charity, and one autograph hunter was quite offended when I wouldn't part with my briar!'

The popularity of the Maigret series continued unabated through the four series of fifty-two episodes screened between 1960 and 1963 – reaching at its peak an audience of 14 million people – and, just as Simenon had anticipated, rights to transmit the stories were enthusiastically snapped up by TV stations all over the world including Australia, Canada, Jamaica, Kenya and many others. The only notable exception was America which had pioneered the inspector on the small screen. Initially, when the series was first being transmitted, the *Radio Times* reported that it had 'attracted considerable attention in America'. But after that all was silence.

The truth about the American refusal to screen the series was a long time in emerging – and when it did, it transpired that the American TV companies had turned down the programme because of what they saw as it's *laissez-faire* attitude towards sex.

When pressed into making a statement about this decision by British journalists, a somewhat embarrassed spokesman in New York said: 'Sexual sin must never be shown to pay. Ladies of easy virtue are shown as quite delightful people and Maigret treats them in too free and easy a manner.'

Despite the undoubted disappointment felt by BBC officials at being unable to break into the world's biggest TV market, the laughter which broke out on hearing this statement echoed all over Television Centre and even through the sets in Studio 3 where all this immorality was supposed to have gone on. (Another complaint the BBC received came from rather closer to home. The British church authorities said they had monitored the series and believed that the number of alcoholic drinks seen consumed in each episode was 'excessive'.)

When the 52nd and final episode of Maigret, *Maigret's Little Joke* was transmitted on Christmas Eve 1963 – almost four years to the day when Basil Sydney had introduced the first inspector to the viewing public – there was a sense of loss and disappointment felt by the public and press alike. A writer in *The Times* probably put it most neatly when he said: 'The feeling of loss is like running out of your favourite cigarettes (French) when the shops are closed.'

The series itself might be over, but the tradition of Maigret on television had been well and truly established. Davies himself was

never to don the inspector's hat or put that famous pipe back into his mouth again on TV, and although the part made him a celebrity, it also undeniably restricted any other roles he might wish to play. That said, his memory remains fresh today long after the vast majority of his contemporaries have been forgotten, and his performance as *le patron* is widely regarded as the benchmark against which all his successors are to be judged.

A scene from the story, 'Death In Mind', with Rupert Davies questioning a suspect, Redek, (Anton Rogers). Transmission was in November 1962.

SIMENON

SIMENON

MAIGRET
IN
COURT

MAIGRET IN COURT

A MEDIOCRE MAIGRET

Philip Mackie's adaptation of *Maigret and the Lady* (Strand) has turned a good-ish detective story into a mediocre play. Maigret, holidaying with his wife in a small Normandy fishing port, is summoned to the home of a morally rotten, *nouveau-pauvre* family where a maid has died of arsenic poisoning after swallowing her mistress's sleeping draught. Joyce Carey is the head of the house, Michael Gough the drunken elder son. There is a good theatrical surprise in the last act when a character thought to be dead walks on to the stage and pours out a glass of Calvados. Otherwise the eveing is a disappointment.

Length is the trouble. The television plays lasted one hour; the dialogue was taut and the action developed swiftly cnough to disguise the awkward fact that Maigret does too much impermissable guesswork. The production at the Strand goes on for two and a half hours, counting intervals, and the faults in construction yawn wide. Something has also happened to the simple, direct style for which Simenon is rightly praised; chunks of the question and answer stuff were no better than plot-fodder.

The justification of all this is the opportunity to see Rupert Davies' gruff, avuncular figure and wrinkled dumpling face in the real. He doesn't come on at the beginning and strike a match against a Watney's wall, but when he does light up, curls of tobacco smoke (genuine Maigret pipe tobacco) waft across the footlights for all to share. It's just a pity he and the rest of the cast weren't given a better play.

Jeremy Kingston,
Punch, 27 October, 1965.

In October 1965 an attempt to repeat the success of Maigret on TV was made with a stage production of Maigret and the Lady *at the Strand Theatre, London, starring Rupert Davies. This cartoon of the star appeared in the souvenir programme. The* Spectator *called the play, 'a poke in the eye with a broken reed' and most audiences shared the disappointment of Jeremy Kingston whose review is reproduced on this page.*

(Opposite) *From the early sixties, Rupert Davies' likeness was to be found on editions of the Simenon novels such as* Maigret In Court *(1961).*

The Italians were the first country to follow the BBC's lead and bring Maigret to their viewers in a series of six, hour-long adaptations which appeared on their screens in the autumn of 1962. Cast as the inspector was the robust and commanding figure of Gino Cervi who had been a familiar face to Italian cinemagoers for many years, but was now to reappear every couple of years or so on TV in a series of six to eight Maigret stories.

Cervi (1901-1974) was born in Bologna, the son of a drama critic, and it was his frequent visits to the theatre as a child which encouraged him to take up acting as a profession. He made his stage debut at twenty-four and became a film star in 1932. A rather larger-than-life character, he proved himself able to play a wide variety of roles ranging from historical figures such as the Emperor Nero and King Carlos of Spain to vaudeville comedians and criminals.

Like serveral of his predecessors in the Maigret role, Cervi appeared in a number of films directed by Julian Duvivier including *The Little World of Don Camillo* (1951) which starred the great Fernandel and also helped make him an international name. In this he appeared as the militant communist mayor, Pepone, and such was the success of the movie, worldwide, that several more of the Don Camillo stories were filmed in succeeding years. It was as a direct result of his popularity in these pictures that Cervi was cast by RAI-TV to star in their Maigret series.

Like the BBC, RAI-TV hoped later to be able to sell their series into the English-speaking market, and it is believed that part of the reason for selecting Cervi was because of his extensive experience of dubbing British and American movies. He had, in fact, dubbed several James Stewart and Sir Laurence Olivier films into Italian, and had done such a good job on Olivier's Shakespearean films that the actor had nicknamed him 'my twin'.

Thick set, silver haired and with a cigarette perpetually at his lips, Cervi had the looks for Maigret and played him as a generally amiable but occasionally explosive *patron*. Alone among all the television Maigrets, he opted to wear the bowler hat and neat dark suit worn by the inspector in the early novels, but was rarely ever seen in an overcoat.

(Opposite) *Gino Cervi, the impressive Italian Maigret, who starred on RAI TV from 1962 to 1973.*

The series began with *Maigret a Pigalle*, a case based on the short story, *Maigret au Picratt's*, about the inspector's dogged pursuit of a sleazy blackmailer, pornographer and murderer. It was a most suitable title for Italian audiences with its mixture of the Pigalle's beautiful girls plus an assortment of wealthy playboys and unscrupulous criminals, all of whom helped give the series a colourful start from which it never looked back.

Cervi played Maigret on Italian TV a total of thirty-six times

over the next decade, as well as extending his law-upholding role by serving as a regional councillor for Lazio from 1970. In January 1974, however, he tragically suffered a stroke while on holiday in Punta Ala, a resort town in the north of Italy, when he was just a few days short of his golden anniversary as an actor. Plans for a further series of Maigret were shelved at that time and have not been revived since.

In most of Cervi's obituaries his appearances as Maigret was given the same prominence as his role in the Don Camillo films. *Variety*, the trade magazine of show business, said in its notice of 23 January 1974: 'Cervi boosted his national popularity even higher as the impersonator of the Gallic hawkeye Maigret, easing up on legit and cinema to spend most of his time portraying the sleuth and receiving a peak audience endorsement percentage of 85 or better'; and *The Times* added: 'He was also well-known as Maigret in a long-running Italian television series based on the books by Simenon.'

A study of his career in *Cine Revue* in 1978 quoted Cervi as saying: 'I enjoyed playing Maigret because there was quite a bit of me in him – inquisitiveness, persistence and a slice of arrogance. In fact, there are several qualities in the commissioner which an actor needs to succeed in this tough business!'

German television followed the lead of the British and Italians with a series starring Heinz Ruhmann which began in 1964 with *Maigret Und Sein Gosster*, based on one of the earliest Simenon novels, *La Dansuese du Gai-Moulin* (*At the Gai-Moulin*, 1931). This is a notable case in which Maigret returns to his creator's birthplace, Liège, to try and solve the murder of a Greek millionaire whose death has implicated a vamp named Adele and her corrupt friend, Rene.

The story also shows Maigret in a rather unusual light as a kind of private detective who runs foul of the Belgian police and at one stage gets himself arrested by them. The inspector even has to resort to a fist fight before he finally solves the murder with 'the deduction of Sherlock Holmes', according to one review of the opening episode.

Ruhmann was at first glance an improbable choice as Maigret. Small of stature, with a rather inconspicuous appearance, he had nonetheless built a career on the deliberate use of these characteristics – in particular playing comedy roles which earned him comparison with Charlie Chaplin. Yet he took readily to the part of the inspector, investing the character with his own blend of quiet but pugnacious determination.

Born in Essen in 1902, Ruhmann was the son and grandson of

hotel owners and was supposed to have followed in this profession. Instead, he quit high school and become a pupil of the producer Fritz Basil in Munich. It was here that he got his first roles playing everything from Shakespeare and Molière to comic parts. In 1930 he made his film debut with the UFA company and became a star in *Die Dret von der Tankstelle*. Another pre-war film also gave him his first taste of the detective story genre when he starred in *Der Mann der Sherlock Holmes War* in 1937.

According to German film historian Friedrich Luft, the Second World War almost destroyed Ruhmann's career. 'He got involved in the dubious business of film production,' Luft wrote, 'and he then had to spend seven years of his life clearing up and paying off his own firm's bankruptcy.'

But from the mid-fifties onwards he revived his career in the cinema with leading roles in the old comedy classic, *Charley's Aunt* (1956), *The Captain from Koepnick* (1956) and *The Good Soldier Schweik* (1960). Luft says that it was 'only late in the day and with justifiable caution' that Ruhmann started to appear on television.

However, his role as Maigret wearing a wry smile beneath a tall felt hat to accentuate his height, proved what a lifetime of hard-won acting experience can enable a good actor to bring to such a

Georges Simenon with four television Maigrets at the unveiling of the statue of his creation at Delfzijl in 1966. They are (from left to right): Rupert Davies (UK); Simenon himself; Heinz Ruhmann (Germany, Jan Teuling (Holland) and Gino Cervi (Italy).

clearly defined role. The German TV critics were particularly impressed by his performances. A columnist in *Stern* wrote: 'Ruhmann knows his métier and calculates his impact. He is small but makes sovereign use of his David-like position and Goliaths inevitably succumb to him. He makes deliberate use of his inconspicuous appearance in order to attract attention on that very account. He also always invites us, very politely, to identify with him.'

The German viewing public certainly identified with Ruhmann and the Maigret stories ran for three seasons, climaxing in 1968 when the star, then nearing seventy but still amazingly spry, appeared in a feature-length screen version of *Maigret Fait Mouche*. Jointly financed by a German and French consortium, the picture was based on the novel *La Danseuse du Gai-Moulin* (1931) and was directed by Alfred Weidmann. It proved an outstanding finale to Ruhmann's term as the Commissaire.

Coinciding with the German Maigret, Dutch TV also began a series featuring the impressive Jan Teuling. A man of commanding physique and expressive, heavy-set features, Teuling chose to wear a white overcoat with a velvet collar similar to the one that Maigret had worn in the early novels, and despite being a non-smoker, still clamped a pipe between his teeth – though alert viewers noticed it was rarely seen alight.

Born in Delft in 1914, Teuling had worked mostly in the theatre until he broke into television in the late fifties. The Maigret series was the first in which he had starred, and a number of the early stories made use of suitable small towns and landscapes in Holland for location shooting. Maigret's office and most indoor scenes, though, were shot in the Amsterdam studios, augmented with crowd and street scenes especially filmed in Paris.

In September 1966, Teuling met Simenon when the author came to Delfzijl, the Dutch seaport where Maigret had been 'born', to unveil a massive bronze statue of the detective. The figure was doubly impressive because just as Simenon had never clearly described Maigret's face in any of the stories about him, so the features of the statue were similarly undefined. It was a day when the universal fame of Maigret was there for all to see and the event earned media coverage around the world – not least because of the five Maigrets who turned up to be introduced and photographed with their creator!

Also present with Teuling were the four other actors who had appeared on television as Maigret: Rupert Davies, Gino Cervi, Heinz Ruhmann and the very latest recruit to this ever-growing band, a Frenchman, Jean Richard.

It was in 1965 that French television had launched its own series of made-for-TV films starring Richard. The series was opened with a sixty-minute adaptation of the 1951 novel, *Maigret en Meuble* (*Maigret Takes a Room*), in which *le patron* investigates two murders committed by an unfortunate man who had returned home after twenty years to find his beloved married. This tragic story of crimes of passion was to be the forerunner of dozens of transmissions throughout the next two decades which would make Richard a household name throughout France. Simenon, however, was not to be numbered amongst his admirers . . .

Richard, born in Paris in 1918, worked in the theatre until the advent of the Second World War and then afterwards went into films and television. Before the Maigret series, he had been best known for starring in the 1960 movie version of the famous French newspaper cartoon series, *La Famille Fenouillard*. This continuing story – which had begun in 1889 – about Agenor Fenouillard, a small town shopkeeper, his imposing spouse, Leocadie, and their two quarrelsome daughters, was the first French comic feature to reach a wide public. In the film, Agenor and Leocadie, with their pretensions of culture and sophistication were played by Richard and Sophie Desmarests.

When the Maigret series featuring Richard was launched, the French press were mixed in their views, but in the following years some notable episodes were screened in which the overall quality of script, acting and production values captured much of the drama and atmosphere of Simenon's original stories. Among those which deserve mention are: *Maigret Hésite* (1968) screened in 1975; *Maigret, Lognon et les Gangsters* (1952) which was shown two years later; *Liberty Bar*, a short story from *Maigret Travels South* (1932) transmitted in 1979; *Maigret à Vichy* (1968) televised in 1984; and *Maigret et le Marchand de Vin* (1970) one of Simenon's last stories about the inspector which was broadcast in 1986.

Although Simenon frequently maintained that he had no interest in watching his creation either in the cinema or on television, he certainly saw at one time or another all the major actors who portrayed him – as an interview given a few years before his death reveals. During the course of this he left his interviewer in no doubt about his views of the various impersonators of Maigret.

'The best three Frenchmen,' he said, 'have been Pierre Renoir, the very first one, because he understood that Maigret was a civil servant and made him behave like one; Michel Simon who, although he played the part only twice, was quite an extraordinary Maigret; and, of course, Jean Gabin, who I don't think ever saw a police commissaire such as Maigret in action and was

really rather too sloppy in his personal appearance with his tie not properly done up and that sort of thing, yet invested the role with his own singular authority. Of the non-French Maigrets, Charles Laughton did his best but was really rather terrible. Gino Cervi, the Italian actor was very good. But it was Rupert Davies, who was really the best – I would put him on a par with Michel Simon.'

Having considered the cinema-Maigrets, Simenon then turned to the current French TV-Maigret.

'Jean Richard may be Maigret for a lot of French people because of all those television films,' he said, 'but for me he is quite honestly the worst. He is very bad. He acts as if he has seen too many American films with gangsters and gigolos. He will arrive at an old lady's or wherever wearing his hat and not take it off. He doesn't say, "Good-morning" but just "Commissaire Maigret". He goes on smoking and keeps his hat on all the time he's there – and he leaves in the same way. That shocked me. A Divisional Commissaire does have a certain amount of education. He knows that you don't visit people with your hat on and smoking a pipe.'

Far away from France, two other countries, the Soviet Union and Japan, also began their own Maigret series. In Russia, the classically-trained stage actor Boris Tenine was cast as the detective in a series which managed to achieve a considerable degree of authenticity despite the fact that the grey and unlovely back streets of Moscow had to 'double' for *le patron*'s Paris. Russian viewers, who had earlier enjoyed a home-made version of the *Adventures of Sherlock Holmes* took to their own version of Maigret with similar enthusiasm.

The Japanese, also great admirers of the sleuth of Baker Street, had similar problems with location when their series was being filmed and had to use the outskirts of Tokyo as a stand-in for the French capital. Nonetheless, the versatile TV actor Kinya Aikawa, with his implacable face and bulky figure, pleased both the critics and public. Simenon apparently saw a couple of episodes of this particular series and is reported to have told some friends that the Japanese actress playing his inspector's wife was 'the best Madame Maigret of them all'.

Only one more actor was to play Maigret on television while Simenon was still alive, and it is very unlikely that he saw this performance at all. The actor was the reformed hell-raising Irishman, Richard Harris, who appeared in a two-hour drama screened on 21 May 1988, entitled, simply, *Maigret*, which, it was hoped by the producer-writer, Arthur Weingarten, would be the first in a line of similar annual productions.

Like Rupert Davies, Harris had not been first choice for this

(Opposite) *Jean Richard has played Maigret on French television at irregular intervals since 1965.*

particular production. It had originally been hoped that Richard Burton would play Maigret, and according to Weingarten, the great Welsh actor had already done some preparatory reading for the role when he died suddenly in August 1984. As a long-time friend of Burton, Harris seemed like a good replacement.

Weingarten, just like the BBC thirty years earlier, said he had been pursuing Simenon for the TV rights for years. In his case, however, it was a writer who helped rather than hindered his mission to secure the author's approval: Graham Greene being a mutual friend who introduced the producer to Simenon.

'He really wasn't anxious to do a deal,' Weingarten recalled later. 'After all he was worth 115 million dollars with royalties of seven or eight million dollars a year. His first words when we started talking business were, "There isn't enough money you can pay me." He was a tough old bird and struck a hard bargain. What made him change his mind was when I offered him something he had never had before – a guaranteed showing in America where his books sell "only" 300,000 copies a year.

'His eyes lit up at that – and once we had made the agreement he didn't want to know what stories we would do or how we would film them or even what changes we proposed to make. He did ask who would play the part, though, and when I told him Richard Harris he said, "I would never have thought of him in a million years." The only other question he asked was how Harris would look. When I told him he would be in old clothes with a duffel coat and hat without a stiffener inside he seemed to be quite happy.'

Weingarten then obtained backing for his project from HTV in Britain and Coca-Cola in America who agreed to a budget of 3 million dollars and location shooting in Paris, the West Country and on board a luxury liner off the Canary Islands. Patrick Drom-goole, the managing director of HTV, and himself a Simenon fan, was enthusiastic about the potential of the project. Speaking in November 1987 he said:

'We are getting sick of "Miami Vice"-style violence. The original Maigret stories were marvellously-crafted detective programmes which had an enriching, noble quality about them. Our programme will be the sort that will bring us back from the direction that "Miami Vice" and the rest have taken us. We need good, intelligent drama with attractive people rather than repulsive ones.'

The production team then set to work on the new Maigret full of optimism. Weingarten's script was drawn from several Maigret novels and relates the story of how the inspector takes a special interest in a case where a former police colleague has been

Richard Harris as the ill-fated Maigret on location for the 1988 HTV production.

murdered on a train and his body hurled into the Seine. The mysterious reasons for this murder are further complicated when Maigret comes into conflict with an American billionaire recluse named Kevin Portman who has just reappeared in public to visit his two sons in Paris, where they run part of his shipping empire, in order to persuade them to sell back their shares in the company.

Despite the film-makers' initial worry that Harris might prove too expensive for their production – or would not want to play Maigret – they soon found themselves talking to a real fan who had long fancied the role: as the actor himself explained later while at work on the picture.

'I had been introduced to Maigret back in 1972 by John Huston,' he said. 'I was instantly hooked and read sixty or seventy of them. It has been an obsession of mine to play him ever since. As I read the stories I became him in my head. The clue to Maigret is that he watches everything, and throws people into psychological confrontations to get their reactions. I also knew exactly how I would look and what I would wear.

'I think they were surprised when I said I would do it. Then they said they couldn't pay my full salary. So I said, "I don't have a salary. There is no price for me. If I like it and you can pay me, fine. If not, I'll still do it because I'll enjoy it."'

These might well have seemed like surprising words from a man who had been born in comparative poverty in Limerick in 1932. After studying for the stage in London, and playing small parts in a number of films, he had become an international star in the award-winning movie *This Sporting Life* in 1963. Several more spectacularly successful films followed which, along with his drinking and womanising, kept him constantly in the headlines. It was, however, a stake in the musical film, *Camelot*, plus a decision to quit drinking in 1981, which subsequently made him, as he put it, 'rich enough to choose what I want to do'.

Harris' appearance as Maigret wearing an ill-fitting suit and cardigan buttoned up the wrong way – in order to make his wiry six-foot frame look bulkier – was not the only liberty taken with the original. The setting was also moved to the 1980s, although the inspector remained essentially a man of the 1950s: avoiding the phone if at all possible and having nothing whatsoever to do with police computers. Harris did, though, want to retain Maigret's shambling walk – and found the solution by wearing size fifteen shoes instead of his normal nine and a half!

'I wanted to invent something totally different from Rupert Davies' Maigret,' he added. 'So I made him a sort of lower middle-class fellow, although I did try to retain Simenon's concept of Maigret as the perfectionist.'

When filming was complete, Harris, twice married, had something interesting to say about Maigret and his single marriage: 'Do you know that in all the Simenon books about the detective, his wife is seldom mentioned and only once by her first name, Louise. He never referred to her by that name. It is always Madame and he was Monsieur, and in all the years they have been married, he never observes the changes in her or in their relationship.

'So in this story while he tries to solve the murder of an old friend, he is also seeking clues to what happened to their marriage. It has soured – like a love affair that has gone to sleep.'

Playing Madame Maigret was Barbara Shelley, famous for a string of roles in Hammer horror movies, with Andrew McCulloch as Sergeant Lucas.

The reception for the production, though, was universally bad. Peter Waymark in *The Times* speaking for the newspapers in general said: 'For those of us who admired Rupert Davies as

Maigret (Richard Harris) with Mme Maigret (Barbara Shelley) in the 1988 HTV production, which moved the original to a contemporary Paris setting.

Cartoonist John Jensen's apt comment on Richard Harris' Maigret. (Punch, 3 June 1988).

Simenon's ruminative, pipe-smoking detective in the BBC Maigret series in the sixties, anyone else attempting the role must seem like an imposter. Even so, Richard Harris seems to have gone out of his way to make his portrayal as least like Davies' as possible. The trouble is that he is not much like Simenon's Maigret either. As played by Harris, he is a big, shambling figure, with a battered hat, glasses, scruffy blonde hair and a croaky Irish accent. Harris even gives him an Irish name, McGrey. He also calls his Peugeot a Pewjo.

'Since most of the other main characters are American, a squabbling family of rich industrialists lifted straight from Dallas/Dynasty, the Frenchness which was the charm and essence of the Simenon stories is all but obliterated. We are left with a conventional and none-too-gripping cop show, with lines like, "Inspector, if you'd like to tell me what this is about . . ." and reaching its finale on a luxury liner which is supposed to be in the sub-tropics but looks as if it is anchored off Skegness in February.'

The *Daily Mail* was one of several other papers whose Letters Page received complaints from readers about the production.

'Why for goodness sake was the action set in modern times?' F. R. Wilson of Orpington in Kent demanded, 'and why did Richard Harris find it necessary to portray Maigret as a shambling, scruffy individual with his trousers hanging down, his shirt hanging out, often wearing his hat back to front and needing a good haircut?

'And in the many Maigret stories which I have read, Madame Maigret rarely refers to him by his first name, but when she does it is as "Jules" and never as "Juley". Also his staff address him as "Patron" and not "Inspector".'

Another reader, Helen Graham from Basingstoke, Hampshire also referred to what she called 'Maigret's French farce' and went on: 'As a travelogue it failed as I noticed none of the exotic backgrounds we were promised. Simenon is dead (sic) otherwise I am sure the author would protest strongly at this truly appalling characterisation of his French detective.'

TV Times received a similarly unhappy postbag, and selected one letter from Joe Wright of St Leonards-on-Sea in Sussex to represent a great many more: 'How could Richard Harris ever have played Maigret as he did after apparently reading Simenon's books? He said that he aimed at something different from the character played by Rupert Davies in the classic TV series. He certainly achieved that – but at what cost! Simenon's books show the detective and his wife as totally rooted in the French way of life. This is the extra dimension – the mysteries are solved because Maigret knows his way round the French character. To project him as a comic Irishman is an absolute betrayal of the life's work of a fine writer.'

The Editor of *TV Times* invited Harris to comment on this letter and the actor replied: 'I have played Maigret in my head for twenty years. Inevitably, my characterisation was different from that played by Rupert Davies in the old TV series which I never saw. But I don't see why an Englishman should be considered more suitable than an Irishman to play a Frenchman.'

Harris' last point was, in fact, a more relevant one than he could have realised at the time. For although he himself has not returned to play Maigret again on television, his successor on British TV, Michael Gambon, is, of course, an Irishman . . .

The year before Gambon's debut as Maigret, however, another new French series was unveiled starring Bruno Cremer, a versatile actor whose fleshy features and bulky figure bore a strong resemblance to the traditional concept of the Commissaire. An interesting connection also emerged between the Granada production and this series by a Paris based-company, Dune, in the shape of their English co-producer, Steve Hawes of Pipeline Films. For Steve had originally been going to work on Granada's *Maigret*, but when the decision was taken to wait for Gambon he decided instead to team up with Dune.

Founded in 1980 by Eve Vercel and Robert Nador, Dune had already made a name as the maker of excellent drama, documentary and entertainment programmes for TV when it began filming the legendary policeman in January 1991. The company has announced an ambitious programme of stories – 104 films in all – each ninety minutes long and all set in the early 1950s. Among the first programmes filmed were *Maigret et les Plaisirs de la Nuit* (written by Jacques Cortal and directed by Jose Pinhero), *Maigret et la Grande Perche* (written and directed by Claude Goretta) and *Maigret chez les Flamands* (written and directed by Serge Leroy) for which the location shooting left Paris for the first time to go to Belgium.

Cremer, a veteran actor who made his screen debut in 1957 in *Quand la Femme S'en Mêle*, has appeared in over fifty movies, including works directed by Costa Gavras (*Un Homme de Trop*, 1967), Luchino Visconti (*Lo Straniero* based on Camus' *L'Etranger* in 1967) and the American director William Friedkin's box office success, *Wages of Fear* (1977). He has also had earlier experience playing a detective in the series, *Les Dossiers de l'Inspecteur Lavardin*. Apart from being an avid reader of the Simenon novels, Cremer also shared a passion with Maigret for pipe smoking and invariably uses his own briars during shooting.

(Opposite and left)
*Bruno Cremer, the
veteran Gallic actor
who has taken on the
mantle of Maigret for
French TV since 1991.*

'It's essential to be true to the original stories to put the real Maigret on the screen,' Cremer said in an interview in 1991. 'So many people have an idea in their head about Maigret that it is important not to disappoint them, although you must bring something of yourself to the role. I think the Commissaire is someone you can go on discovering things about for as long as you choose to play him.'

Appearing with Cremer as his inspectors are the 'big-hearted, innocent giant' Torrence, played by Serge Beauvois, and the patient 'little Janvier', Jean-Claude Frissung. Among the guest stars to have appeared in the early episodes are Alexis Nitzer, Renee Faure and Michael Lonsdale, the French born son of an Englishman.

Jose Pinhero, who directed the first of the Cremer episodes commented succinctly as the series opened on French TV: 'Maigret is more than just a character now. He is an institution. And of how many other characters from twentieth-century fiction can we say that?'

4

MAIGRET'S PARIS . . . IN BUDAPEST

DUSK IS FALLING AND the sign above the Moulin Rouge is already glowing a deep crimson against the dark blue skyline. The boulevard in front of the famous theatre is crowded with men and women in wide-shouldered suits and dresses with nipped waists, some of them stepping smartly between the steady flow of cars sputtering their exhausts into the evening air. Insistent horns and the occasional command of a *gendarme* on point duty add to the noise of a great city awakening to the pleasures of the night.

Across the square, in front of some advertisements for Disque Bleu and Dubonnet, a number of people are filing in and out of the entrance to the Metro, while the last of some flea market stall-holders are closing up for the day. Several of the nearby cafés are already a-buzz with the conversation of early diners as well as the enticing sounds of food being prepared.

In front of one of these Brasseries, a strangely familiar car, a black, low-slung Citroën Traction-Avant with an inverted chrome V on its radiator, pulls up at the kerb and two men step out. They approach an even more familiar figure sitting slightly hunched at one of the tables. He is wearing a trilby hat and trench coat over a dark blue, three-piece suit. He sits smoking a pipe and staring reflectively into a *demi*, a half pint of beer. Beside him lies an open note book in which are scribbled a number of names and dates. The man is a policeman and he is on the hunt for a killer . . .

At first glance, the setting seems just like one of the most familiar in the world: Paris in the fifties as it was so often photographed by the great Henri Cartier-Bresson. Yet appearances can be deceptive – for we are, indeed, many hundreds of miles from the French capital. In fact, this is a downtown part of Budapest, the capital city of Hungary.

Nor does the deception end there. For the man sitting at the table is not actually French, nor is he a policeman, but the actor Michael Gambon, the latest man to take on the role of the lugubrious, gentle, yet quietly menacing Chief Inspector Maigret. The two men who have arrived to see him are actors, too, playing the Commissaire's assistants Sergeant Lucas and Inspector Janvier (Geoffrey Hutchings and Jack Galloway). As the three men converse, the cameras on the pavement to their right turn over under the watchful eye of the director, James Cellan-Jones, and his crew.

Two minutes later, the lights on the façade of the Moulin Rouge flicker out, the pedestrians stop their animated bustle, and another scene for Granada Television's new Maigret series is over. Actors and technicians once again mingle outside the opera house where TV cabins have been set up for the location, and the handful of members of the public who politely paused to let the scene be shot, move on – picking their way carefully over a tangle of thick electric cables lying along the street.

Just around the corner, in the adjoining main street of Andrassy ut – known to most English visitors as the Oxford Street of Budapest – life continues as if nothing unusual at all had happened. The sound of a number 6 tram clanks by, and, amidst the general hubbub of modern cars, men and women in the fashions of the nineties go about their evening pursuits.

The magic of the film camera and the ingenuity of the men and women of television are once again being used to bring to life some of Simenon's famous detective stories. But this September evening in 1991 is a far cry from the day when Granada Television decided to become the latest company to adapt the unmistakable Maigret for the small screen. The story of that decision and how it became reality is a fascinating one . . .

It was the unprecedented public and press acclaim that has surrounded Granada's production of *The Adventures of Sherlock Holmes* in the years since its launch in 1984 that set the company searching the crime shelves for another literary detective to adapt for the nation's screens. The hallmarks of the Holmes series – which stars Jeremy Brett as the Great Detective (initially with David Burke as his faithful chronicler, Dr Watson, and subsequently, Edward Hardwicke) – have been a painstaking attention to period detail, authentic dialogue and locations which perfectly recreated the late-Victorian period of the original stories written by Sir Arthur Conan Doyle. The result is a programme that has been hailed around the world and is still generating new adventures a decade later.

After considering dozens of detectives and hundreds of books, the choice of Maigret to be given the same treatment as Holmes was one fraught with as many problems as possibilities. First, there was the inevitable fact that whoever filled the role of *le patron* would immediately be compared by all older viewers to Rupert Davies. Secondly, if the series was to be faithful to Simenon's original stories, how much remained of the Paris that he had so evocatively written about? And, thirdly, how would audiences used to the all-action, often-violent exploits of TV's current crop of detectives take to a central character who preferred public transport to fast police cars; whose methods involved brain power rather than brawn; and who preferred to solve his cases over a pipe and a glass of beer while his lieutenants did the leg work?

David Plowright, Granada's much respected Chairman, was the man who had to take the final decision of committing 3 million pounds to a six-part series. In some ways the decision paralleled the one he had faced with Sherlock Holmes back in 1983. Then he knew that Jeremy Brett was taking on a role that to many members of the public was firmly associated with either Basil Rathbone in the cinema or Peter Cushing on television. He knew, too, that Holmes' London was a thing of the past and would have to be recreated, and, perhaps most crucial of all, that the eccentric nineteenth-century Baker Street detective was being asked to follow in the footsteps of such international successes as the lollipop-sucking New York Lieutenant Kojak or the pair of abrasive young Los Angeles plainclothes cops, Starksy and Hutch.

Plowright's decision to take that gamble resulted in a definitive performance by Brett as Holmes; a Baker Street set (adjacent, incidentally, to Granada's Coronation Street set in their Manchester studios) and a series of locations primarily in Lancashire and Cheshire that positively exuded Victorian England. Indeed, it created a series of such compelling authenticity that it opened up a whole new genre for cerebral detectives on television.

The job of bringing the legendary Maigret to the screen became the task of the energetic and experienced producer, Jonathan Alwyn, who never had a moment's doubt about the potential of the series.

'Maigret is part of detective folklore,' he said when taking on the job, and reaffirms today. 'I believed right from the start that there was a whole generation of viewers who were much too young to have seen the BBC series.'

It was a statement mixcd with some poignancy for Alwyn, because he had been a friend of Rupert Davies and had been saddened by the fact that, after all his success with Maigret, Davies rarely worked again, so identified had he become with the role.

'I remember what he said not long before his death,' Alwyn reminisces, pulling on a pipe similar to the one Davies – and Maigret – smoked. 'He said, "I didn't have a life as an actor after I put on his trilby and struck that match against a wall at the opening of every episode."'

Despite this, Alwyn was more than a little pleased by a message he received after it was announced that Granada were going to re-make Maigret. It was a good luck message from Davies' widow, Jessica, from her home in Pistyll, Gwynedd, and said: 'I am delighted you are going to make the series. It will be difficult to play the part as well as Rupert. I have always thought it a shame that Rupert's series was made just before colour came in or it would have been repeated many times.'

Both Plowright and Alwyn knew only too well that their most crucial decision was choosing the right actor to play Maigret — that, and finding the locations in which to set the stories. The first choice proved the easier of the two for both had seen Michael Gambon in his award-winning role in Dennis Potter's television series, *The Singing Detective*, and agreed that *he* was the man. The only problem was that Gambon's other theatrical commitments meant he would not be available to play the role for eighteen months. But Granada had waited a year for Jeremy Brett under similar circumstances and the outcome had exceeded all their expectations. They would stick by the decision and in the meantime the production team would turn their attention to the location.

It needed only one visit to Paris to discover that the city of the fifties — in which Granada had decided to set the stories — had gone.

Of course, it is no more true that Maigret actually walked the streets of Paris in search of criminals than Holmes and Watson sought their prey in late-nineteenth-century London. But Simenon knew the city intimately and consequently was able to relate graphically the Commissaire's cases against a background of Parisian life at its most ordinary. He did this in such a way that millions of readers all over the world who had never been near the place 'saw' it through his eyes. He also imprinted the stolid figure of the detective on a number of French landscapes — in particular, watery northern ones — so that they, too, sprang unforgettably from the printed page.

Sadly, though, time has taken its toll of Maigret's Paris. Modern apartment blocks and a six-lane auto-route have obliterated the run-down tenements, sleazy bars and dance halls of Charenton where the Marne joins the Seine. The Marais, too, where Simenon himself lived as a young man had been scoured of its colourful low-life, which may well have saved its historical and architectural elements, but has deprived the area of the seething humanity who were very much *le patron*'s people.

Naturally, one or two of Maigret's haunts have survived. In the Place Dauphine on the tip of the Ile de la Cité, with the Seine run-

The real Paris of the fifties . . .

ning briskly on either side, the Restaurant Paul still stands invitingly. It was to this 100-year-old bastion of plain French cooking – renamed the Brasserie Dauphine in Simenon's stories – that Maigret liked to adjourn for lunch with Lucas and Janvier, after the trio had first enjoyed a quick Pernod at the zinc bar. Behind the varnished brown paint of the restaurant's front, in a far corner looking out over the quay, is the table at which the Commissaire sat. On many days of the week the spot takes on something of the air of a shrine as tourists from all the corners of the world mingle silently outside and peep in for a view.

A short walk away on the Quai des Orfèvres is Maigret's office in the Judiciaire which has been described as Paris' Scotland Yard. It was here in a room overlooking the Seine that he would select one of the fifteen pipes hanging in his wall rack and, billowing smoke, ponder the clues brought to him about the latest murder. Today's policemen working in the Orfèvres apparently no longer adjourn for lunches at Restaurant Paul – or, indeed, ring for a waiter to bring up plates of sandwiches and *demis* of beer while they work on sifting clues. Instead, impersonal vending machines ranged along the corridors filled with soft drinks and snacks have replaced even those modest pleasures.

Much as he loves Paris, Alwyn knew there was no way he could film his new Maigret series in the city.

'The settings were contemporary for the BBC version,' he explains, 'but we had to approach Maigret as a period piece. Paris is now substantially different from the fifties. It's been cleaned up and invaded by tourists. And it's so frenetic.

'It is still the most beautiful city, but apart from the problems with tourists, there is also the traffic and the roadsigns. It would have been difficult and very expensive to get the facilities and co-operation we required. So we had to look elsewhere.'

The Granada researchers in fact scouted several of the older European capitals, and for a while Brussels was pencilled in as a possible location. But once the first reports came back from Budapest, the choice settled itself. There was at least one very good omen, too. Much of the city had been built in the late nineteenth century by architects inspired by Baron Haussmann, the creator of modern Paris.

While most other major European cities have undergone face-lifts in recent years, Budapest has retained its post-war atmosphere and there is a feeling of intrigue engendered during the Nazi occupation and the days of the Cold War still hanging in its streets. In the cafés and restaurants, people still sit lingering away the time over newspapers while drinking strong coffee and brandy, or else eating rich, steaming dishes and fresh, warm pastries that would tempt the Commissaire himself. It is all so immediately reminiscent of Maigret's Paris.

Although there are also numerous signs of Western influence to be found such as the ubiquitous Burger King restaurants and shops along the main shopping street, the Vaci utca (the Bond Street of Budapest) selling everything from Stefanel fashions to compact disc players, the visitor needs only to turn into a side street and the clock has stopped half a century ago. The mixture of tall, dark buildings with their art deco ironwork, the pavement stalls in dark, crumbling alleys, plus the plentiful taxis and cheap public transport, make it easy to see why the city has earned its reputation of 'the Paris of Central Europe'.

When Alwyn visited Budapest he was immediately impressed. 'First there was the architecture of the place which had been influenced by Haussman's designs for Paris,' he recalls, 'and the fact that it still had that shabby, intimate atmosphere, pock-marked walls and so on – an echo of what post-war Paris was like.

'Secondly, there was the attitude of the Budapest authorities. They were so enthusiastic about the whole project. They were happy to close down whole streets for us and let us put up posters for Dubonnet and Disque Bleu. If we told them, ''That street sign must go'', they just took it down. We got the street names and

Maigret's Brasserie Dauphine in Budapest, 1993.

A Budapest street transformed into 1950s' Paris for the Maigret *series.*

Metro signs made locally, but we had to bring in the old Citroën cars from France and Czechoslovakia. About the only other things we had to import were cockles and mussels from Germany and seaweed from England for the seaside scenes!

'The local people were marvellous,' He adds. 'They didn't bother us at all, some of them didn't even seem to notice what we were doing. When you film in London, the world and his wife come to watch, but in Budapest we scarcely got any interest from the public.'

Transforming the square behind the Andrassy ut into Maigret's patch with café exteriors, a flea market and Metro station was carried out with remarkable efficiency with the aid of local crafts-men, creating in a matter of weeks a suitable Gallic atmosphere that made it very hard to tell the Danube from the Seine. If being in Budapest meant there would be none of the usual 'travel bro-chure' views of Paris, this was not something that unduly worried Alwyn.

'You really don't need the Eiffel Tower rammed up people's noses every five minutes,' he jokes.

Of course not all of the episodes could be shot in Budapest, and much of the rest of the location shooting was done outside the city in the countryside at a place called Nadasdladanyi Kastelyi. Here a once magnificent mansion which had been appropriated by the State after the Second World War was transformed into a French château. Inside, the props department hung crystal chan-deliers, filled a library with books and added a nice touch with an old wind-up gramophone to give the place everything but the smell of Paris.

A barn on the mansion's estate was also converted into a French home – false walls covered with period wallpaper being introduced to complete the effect. Three small villages nearby were selected for scenes in the episode *Maigret on Home Ground*, in which the Chief Inspector's investigations took him back to the village where he had grown up.

Apart from this painstaking attention to detail, Alwyn was equally anxious that the series should capture the subtle and muted quality of the original stories, both in terms of the scripts and the photography.

'We were very fortunate to get the Oscar-winning Hungarian cameraman Elemer Ragalyi to work on the series,' he says. 'I told him I wanted it to be like a black and white film that happens to be shot in colour. I think he achieved that superbly.'

The writers of the opening episodes were also thoroughgoing professionals such as Robin Chapman and Alan Plater who had both worked on Granada's Sherlock Holmes series.

'Of course Maigret is steeped in nostalgia for a Paris that no longer exists,' explains Plater, who adapted the first story in the series, the ninety-minute special, *The Patience of Maigret*. 'Which lays us open to the charge about TV drama being backward looking. But Maigret is done in a way that Granada perfected in the Sherlock Holmes series – with an invisible wink to the audience – so that they know it's meant to be a dream of Paris and a dream of a detective.'

To underline the mood of the films, Alwyn instructed his script-writers to avoid using flowery Frenchisms – to use terms such as 'Monsieur le' and 'Comte d' only when absolutely necessary and no broken accents whatsoever.

'I wanted the stories to be quieter than the usual frenetic detective stories you see on television,' he says. 'There are fairly long dialogues between characters in Simenon's books and I believe they are part of the essence of Maigret. That's what I wanted on the screen, too.'

Filming was not, of course, without its problems. There was always the language barrier, and the Hungarian weather had a tendency to change at a crucial moment. Then it was a matter of joining the locals huddled in a nearby café sipping black coffee. The Café Muvesz close by the location proved a favourite with the Granada team – not least because of the cheerful, white-booted waitresses!

Being a series about crime, it was perhaps not altogether surprising that the film crew found themselves at one stage the target of some small time local crooks.

'These black market con men would come sidling up to our chaps and offer to change money,' Alwyn remembers with a rueful smile. 'But the thing was when you got the cash, you'd find the buggers had wrapped a genuine note around a wad of paper.'

The one person who avoided falling into this trap – though he was aware of the con men – was Michael Gambon who, when not on camera, was doing his famous 'invisible man' act. He might be the star of the series, but Gambon is an actor who does not relish interviews and keeps his private life very private indeed. He was actually pleased on the day during shooting when some tourists from Devon inquired of a production assistant who the star was and when told said, 'Michael who?'

'I don't mind not being known in the least,' he says without any trace of false modesty. 'If you want to convince people on stage or on film, the less they know about you the better.'

Indeed, piecing together the life of Gambon and his approach to the job of acting and playing Maigret in particular, demands the investigative powers of the Chief Inspector himself. But the results reveal a perceptive and deeply committed actor who has well-justified Granada's decision to wait all those months in order that he might become what an increasing number of people now believe to be very close to a definitive Maigret . . .

If ever there was an actor who physically fitted the popular conception of Maigret it is most probably Michael Gambon. He is a heavily-built, powerful man with long, demonstrative arms, who stands over 6 foot tall and wears size 12 shoes. He is thinning on top and sports a small, pale moustache. He has the shambling walk, lugubrious face and kind of gentle, self-mocking manner that perfectly suits that of the Chief Inspector. His malleable features – he once described his face as being like 'a balloon full of hot water' – and surprisingly mild voice are equally ideal for a character who is famous for his ability to listen to, and empathise with, suspects (although there is a resonance that hints at great depths).

No one should be fooled, though, by his bland, bulky face with its grey, heavy-lidded eyes, because they mask a quick wit and intelligence, also like that of the man he is now impersonating. Despite his massive, ungainly presence, Gambon is adept and moves quickly on his feet when the need arises. Maigret has an intuition for doing what he must do, and Gambon's life has likewise been about doing, intuitively, that which would further his career.

When he can be enticed into talking about himself and his life, Gambon mingles his conversation in the slow, flat tones of south London with a juicy laugh that one journalist has described as 'gurgling like a hot poker in a mug of beer'. He is often informal and deadpan, but can also be unpredictable, anarchic and let fly with a Rabelaisian joke or curse. His voice and his manner are, indeed, a far cry from his humble Irish origins.

Michael John Gambon was born in Dublin on 19th October 1940, the eldest of Edward and Mary Gambon's three children. The family was working class, though Michael believes that the name is of Spanish derivation, brought to the Irish coast during the days of the Spanish Armada. It is a mystery that intrigues him, as does the fact that not one of his forebears did anything remotely artistic.

He has few memories of Ireland, except that his father was a soldier in the army of the Irish Free State from the age of twenty-one. At the beginning of the Second World War, Edward Gambon came to London and served as a war reserve policeman during the Blitz. In 1945, the rest of the family joined him and they all settled in Camden Town.

Michael, though, has rather stronger memories of serving as an altar boy at St Aloysius Catholic Church, and this he believes gave him his first theatrical experience.

'It had a lot of mystery to it,' he recalls. 'Dressing up in all that lovely gear and walking out in front of the congregation. Saying the Latin Mass with the Priest. And that marvellous smell of incense. It was all magical. That might well be the beginnings of my acting.'

He left school at fifteen and first swept floors and made the tea at a factory manufacturing radios and televisions sets. At sixteen he secured a job as an apprentice toolmaker at Vickers Armstrong who made everything from shot guns to sewing machines. The job gave him a delight in precision engineering which he has never lost. He also became fascinated with antique guns – an interest that was fostered by his father who frequently brought home firearms and swords he had bought at markets and hung on the walls of his son's bedroom. His fascination continues to this day.

'Antique guns are my primary passion after acting,' he admits. 'I love them as objects of engineering and design. I have no interest in modern, mass-produced guns – I think they are horrible things. With me, it's the craftsmanship, the form, the line.'

Gambon restores guns for his collection in his workshop at home whenever the demands of his career allow him the time. He never fires the guns he works on, although when he has finished with them they are in working order. He has perfected the art of etching and engraves beautiful designs on them, too. He says that he learned about guns the way he learned acting – by teaching himself.

His introduction to the stage came at the age of seventeen when he happened to walk past the Erith Playhouse one day and saw a sign reading, 'Backstage Help Required'. He volunteered, and because of his mechanical aptitude proved himself a more than accomplished set-builder. Then, seeking to emulate his movie hero, James Dean, he agreed to take on a bit part in a play called *Orange Blossom*.

'The moment I got on stage I just went varoom,' he says. 'I thought, Jesus, this is for me. I want to be an actor.'

During the next few years he combined his apprenticeship by day with appearing in amateur theatricals at night until, aged twenty-one, he decided to write to Michael Mac Liammoir at the

Gate Theatre in Dublin for an audition. He chose the Gate because he once recalled walking past the theatre as a child. Although his curriculum vitae contained a number of credits that were wholly fictitious, he admits now, he was offered a job. He made his professional debut at the age of twenty-two as the second gentleman of Cyprus in *Othello*. His role consisted of standing silently on stage carrying a spear.

In 1963, he landed a job as a founder member of Laurence Olivier's first company at the National Theatre. He found himself spear-carrying again, but this time in very good company. With Anthony Hopkins, Robert Stephens and Derek Jacobi, Gambon began to learn his craft. Then on the advice of Olivier that he needed to gain more experience, he went to Birmingham Rep where he was shortly afterwards spotted by a BBC producer and entered the world of television. For the next two years he had a major role in *The Borderers*, a swashbuckling series set in the Highlands. The bizarre situation of an Irishman playing a Scot was not lost on him! It did, though, convince him of the variety of roles he was capable of playing and this was followed by a number of classical Shakespearean parts.

Michael Gambon on location in the countryside near Budapest for the episode 'Maigret Goes To School'.

Apart from appearing in *King Lear*, *Antony & Cleopatra* and *Uncle Vanya*, he also played in Brecht's *Galileo*, a part that had been brought to the stage by Charles Laughton, an earlier Maigret. Gambon was applauded by the actors as well as the public for his commanding performance in this role. Sir Ralph Richardson even went so far as to call him, 'The Great Gambon' – 'In the curious sense,' Gambon believes, 'maybe he saw me as slightly grotesque?' Others think it was an acknowledgement of a man destined to become one of the country's leading modern actors.

Gambon's stage breakthrough as far as the general public was concerned came in 1974 playing Tom the vet in Alan Ayckbourn's *The Norman Conquests* in the West End. It was to prove the first of a continuing relationship with Ayckbourn and his black comedies – two of the productions, *A Chorus of Disapproval* and *Man Of The Moment*, earning him the particularly sweet triumphs of Olivier awards. It was, indeed, his superlative performance as Douglas, a chinless clerk who once, quite untypically, foiled a bank raid by tackling a raider with a shotgun, and is then confronted seventeen years later by the robber who has become an obnoxious chat show host (played by Peter Bowles) that provided him with another West End hit and also prevented him from starting filming Maigret for eighteen months.

For television audiences, however, it was his performance in Dennis Potter's *The Singing Detective* in 1986 that made him a household name. It was the part that first introduced him to the life of a detective – albeit one who was hospitalised and suffering from the unpleasant skin condition of psoriasis. His role as Philip Marlow in the series, which attracted a viewing audience of over 8 million, was nominated Best TV Drama of the Year by the Broadcasting Press Guild, and won Gambon a BAFTA award. And despite appearing under horrendous make-up consisting of cracked skin and scabs, the series brought him over 300 fan letters.

He particularly remembers working on the series for the looks of horror that invariably appeared on the faces of extras whenever he came on set to play a scene – and the practical joke he played on his co-star, Joanna Whalley, as Nurse Mills.

'I spray-painted the outline of suspenders and fishnets around my vital parts,' he says, a smile breaking out across his face. 'Well, when she pulled back the covers to anoint my aching body you can just imagine! She had screaming hysterics. You can do that sort of thing in films when its only a camera rehearsal.'

Gambon has something of a reputation as a clown in his profession and has pulled numerous practical jokes on fellow actors – some of which he admits to and others which are darkly attributed to him by offended parties unable to take the joke. Though he is very serious about his art, there is no disguising he also has a very subversive sense of humour.

Referring again to *The Singing Detective*, he adds: 'Filming is an acquired skill I didn't have for quite a while. That series broke the ice for me. I was in front of the camera for seven months – it was like acting to a mate. It made me feel much more relaxed about television.'

His sense of humour surfaces once again at the thought. 'Because I smoke cigarettes I thought at one time I might like to do an advert for them if I could use the Singing Detective persona. The trouble is they've banned cigarette ads – but wouldn't he be perfect for those ads. "You're Never Alone With a Strand"!'

When Gambon is asked why he decided to take the role of Maigret his more flippant answers include, 'The size of the part' and 'For the money'. But when he addresses the question seriously the answer is rather different.

'I'd been doing a lot of stage work, which is mentally and physically exhausting,' he says quietly, 'and I wanted to do a popular TV series. I've never done much "popular" stuff, so that was my motivation. I've always been "upmarket".

'Mind you, I am wary of TV fame. I don't quite know why, but I'd rather have theatre fame than TV fame. Television is almost too easy to watch – it just sits there in the corner and you can turn it on and off without any effort.

'In the theatre, people have paid hard cash and you know they're really watching. Theatre is harder than working at the coal face. I've always lacked confidence in my face in front of the cameras. It's quite a useful face for the stage, though, because it's big and people can see it.'

In making his decision, had Gambon given any thought to what a hard act he was being asked to follow? In particular his television predecessor, Rupert Davies who, it was said, was dogged by the shadow of his own success and when he died from cancer at the age of fifty-nine was penniless, disillusioned and out of work – despite having been paid a reputed £1,000 per episode. Or, indeed, any of the *other* actors who had preceded him in the cinema?

'I didn't give a second thought to the others who had played the role.' he says bluntly. 'I certainly don't believe playing Maigret will ruin my career, and I'm too old to worry about being typecast. Anyhow, it's different these days. Look at John Thaw. He

was in *The Sweeney*, then *Inspector Morse*, and more recently in *Stanley and the Women*. Playing one detective hasn't ruined his career and he's got no worries about dying penniless.'

In fact, Michael approached the role with very little knowledge of Maigret or Simenon's books about him. 'I was in my twenties when the Rupert Davies series was on and I didn't watch much television then. I hadn't read any of the books and all I knew about Simenon was that he was supposed to have made love to 10,000 women. What a bloke. It's a wonder he had time to write at all!

'All I really had were a few dim memories of the series. Before I started filming I did see one of the Davies episodes and it seemed very stilted to me. Maigret came across like a benign family doctor, although he does have a dry wit.'

So how had he approached the part?

'It's very simple. The only way to get inside a character like Maigret is to start with the script. That's how you find him, by what he says and how he's described. You know he smokes a pipe. You know he's married, takes the Metro to work, likes a drink, that he's humorous and gets on well with criminals. Once you get an idea how Maigret feels then you can start acting like him.'

Gambon spent four extremely demanding months in Hungary working almost every day to make the first series and returned with some very definite ideas about the Chief Inspector, whom he believes to be 'one of the classic characters of detective fiction – a very human creation'. However, he confesses that one element of the character evades him.

'I still don't know what his face is like,' he says, 'only his presence. He's burly, neatly dressed and stands with his feet slightly apart. He is a man with natural authority surrounded by his loyal detectives who offer him alert obedience. He likes his work and he likes criminals. He finds good people boring. He pretends to be a lot vaguer than he is. He's a good man, compassionate, a bit of a social worker. And he has quite a sense of humour – at least, he has one now. He's no more complicated than that.

'In fact, I suppose Maigret is everyone's dream detective,' he adds. 'He holds his cards close to his chest. He's never in a rush, but he gets results. I'm sure no one like him exists in real life.'

Gambon thinks that Maigret – who he sometimes mischievously refers to in conversation as either 'Migraine' or 'Margaret' – is different from most other detectives on television in that he doesn't ask many questions.

'He is quite economical with them, in fact. But he has a deep

(Opposite) *Maigret (Michael Gambon) with Mme Maigret (Barbara Flynn).*

knowledge of the criminal mind. He seems so straightforward, but he's very perceptive. He's a good listener with a nose for truth and for people. He susses them out by what they don't say as well as what they do.

'On the surface he can be almost childlike and he uses that quality to get through to people. Occasionally he can be a bit threatening but he seldom loses his temper. There is a barrier with people other than his wife because he doesn't want to reveal himself too much.'

Gambon could be talking of himself as he speaks, and he does not deny that he has put quite a lot of himself into the role – as he invariably does with any part. One thing he did find a problem, though, was smoking Maigret's pipe.

'Viewers may have noticed that Maigret doesn't smoke as much as he did. I tend to light up the pipe and then drop it or pop it in my top pocket.'

Pipe-smoking producer Alwyn revealed that although Gambon is a cigarette smoker, 'He hated the pipe. He just doesn't share the Chief Inspector's passion for strong, black tobacco, and he actually turned green at the first couple of attempts at lighting the pipe.'

Gambon did accept that the pipe was an essential prop and disguised his discomfort. 'It's a ruminating thing. You can trust a man who smokes a pipe. It's a sign of power and dignity. But I wasn't converted. I kept it out of shot whenever possible.'

He would, though, have liked to have seen a little more action in some of the stories, perhaps even a car chase. 'But that's not what Maigret is about, I know,' he says. 'He solves the crime, but is always gentle about it. He never condemns the criminal – he likes them. Really, he is always slightly reluctant to rock the boat.'

Gambon was pleased about the producer's policy of avoiding broken English accents or Franglaise in the scripts. But he had to listen to a French actor reading the lines in order to learn the spoken French words.

'It was a bit of a slog because I don't speak the language at all and the odd French word in a script can throw me out of my rhythm like riding a bike over a bump. I believe it would have been disastrous to introduce the Inspector Clouseau kind of accents unless you wanted to make the whole series comic. Of course, it might have been a hit like 'Allo, 'Allo'!

If speaking the odd word of French was not easy, how did he cope with trying to pretend he was in France when, in fact, the cast was working in Hungary?

'We thought about Paris all the time while we were filming

because we were concerned that it should look and feel French. I certainly believe the series has the atmosphere of fifties' Paris,' he replies.

As to the reason for the public's fascination with the stories both on the printed page and the screen, Gambon sees the explanation for this quite clearly.

'Everybody loves whodunits. They all have their own momentum. And the Maigret cases are not like modern detective stories, which are all flawless with forensic. They have a charm about them. Maigret never seems to hit anybody. He doesn't shoot guns. He puffs on his pipe and thinks a lot. He doesn't do much. But then I don't suppose many detectives do. I know one or two and I know they don't!'

The grin which spreads across Gambon's face enlarges still further when it is suggested that the success of Maigret might turn him into a sex symbol with women viewers like Morse's and Van der Valk's.

'Me, a sex symbol,' he muses. 'So women like old boys? I know Simenon based Maigret on himself, although he isn't a womaniser. He's a comforting figure, isn't he? You know you're safe with him. He's got a sense of humour, too, and women always fall for a man who makes them laugh. That's probably the secret of his appeal. But I've never been called a sex symbol before. I've always been covered in make-up playing old monsters such as Lear or Othello. But I do get fan letters – and some of them are from women. Who would have thought it?'

In between making the first and second series of Maigret, Gambon enjoyed a complete change of character by playing a hardened criminal.

'I've been the luckiest man in the world where my roles are concerned. You see I've never really planned anything. I've now played vicious criminals as well as policemen. After Maigret I went to Hollywood to appear in *Mobsters* playing a Mafia boss who cut a man's throat from ear to ear. I got chucked out of the top storey of a skyscraper and had to go screaming down to death. It was terrific. The year before that I was in New York for a film in which Sean Penn shot me through the head. That was good, too. Even in Shakespeare I'm usually cast as the villain.'

For many cinemagoers, Gambon's most memorable criminal role was as the dangerous and obnoxious master crook, Albert, with his pretentions to culture, in Peter Greenaway's film, *The Cook, The Thief, His Wife and Her Lover*.

'I was attracted to the idea of playing someone who does not have much good in him,' he explains. 'Albert is a bad man,

The Granada crew in production with a vintage Citroën.

although he obviously loves his wife, which I suppose goes some way towards explaining his behaviour. I've certainly never met anyone like him.'

When he is not working Gambon lives unostentatiously in south-east London. To get away from all thoughts of work he has a private pilot's licence and likes to fly a Piper Cherokee. He has now almost thirty years flying experience in his log book.

One of his favourite routes is from London to Ipswich because it is a route with which he is familiar. 'Otherwise I'd get lost!' he says. Once again serious he adds: 'I don't fly to relax because you have to concentrate so much when you are up in the air. You can't sit back when piloting a plane. What I like is the technology of flying. I like the instruments. When you fly you have to focus every second.'

But he can still play the practical joker in the air. He once took up a fellow actor, promising to cure him of his fear of flying. He levelled out at 2,000 feet and just when his companion seemed to be about to relax, he faked a heart attack and put the plane into a steep dive.

'It was very cruel, but I couldn't resist it,' he confesses. 'The poor guy was panic-stricken. He just sat there rigid in his seat. When I stopped having the attack and pulled out of the dive he just said two words to me. One of them was very rude!'

Michael would like to own a plane of his own, but believes he is too erratic as well as being disorganised financially.

'Buying a plane would mean doing Maigret for ever,' he says. 'I find it exciting not knowing what I'll be doing next. An actor

Michael Gambon, photographed on the set of the Commissaire's office, has perfected the art of appearing to smoke a pipe!

could be well off on Maigret alone. It would certainly give me the financial rewards, but the risks are too high. I wouldn't want to wear the same trilby and three piece suit for the rest of my life. With long running parts, as Maigret could become, you bend them to you – you put yourself into a character and make him do all the things you do yourself.

'To put it simply, I just read the script, do the stuff, and let the viewers make up their minds. This Maigret is basically *me*.'

The Maigret which Gambon presented to TV audiences for the first time in February 1992 was certainly one they recognised and enjoyed. As did the reviewers of the national press.

The series was launched on Sunday evening, 9 February with Alan Plater's ninety-minute special, *The Patience of Maigret*, in which the Chief Inspector uncovers a complex web of relationships following the murder of gangster Manuel Palmari, a suspected jewellery thief. Geoffrey Hobbs in that morning's *Mail on Sunday* declared enthusiastically:

'Prepare to meet the ultimate Gallic "flic", Chief Inspector Maigret, Mark II (sic) . . . Michael Gambon makes an arresting debut. He's the kind of actor who can convey more drama in a Gallic shrug than most screen cops manage to inject into a gun battle.'

The Times, the next morning, also hailed the debut of Maigret: 'one of the great fictional sleuths of the century played with characteristic intensity by Michael Gambon'; *The Daily Telegraph* likewise enthused: 'Gambon is terrific as Maigret. His great quality is to fill the screen without appearing to, just as Maigret quietly subsumes all the characters into himself in order to "understand the drama".'

The reviewers also praised the performances of the Chief Inspector's 'trusty sidekicks': Geoffrey Hutchings as Sergeant Lucas, Jack Galloway as Inspector Janvier and James Larkin as Lapointe. The delightful Ciaran Madden was singled out, too, for her 'charming cameo' as Mme Maigret. The *Daily Express* even had a word for the background: 'The French locations are authentically atmospheric – no mean feat for an Anglo-Hungarian production filmed in Budapest.'

Interestingly, too, as the series continued, the *Daily Mail* reported that Maigret's classic Citroën Traction-Avant car was making as big an impact on TV viewers as Bergerac's Triumph Roadster and Morse's Jaguar. A dealer who had supplied some of the cars for the series was said to be planning to open more branches of his company in order to meet public demand for the vintage cars which were selling at between £5,000 and £6,000.

The remaining five stories of the series – each an hour long – confirmed the appeal of the programme and the stature of Gambon in the title role. John Junor, the forthright columnist of the *Mail on Sunday*, had this to say as the first series drew to a close:

'It is with a sense of utter bliss that I settle down in the armchair these Sunday nights to watch Maigret on ITV. Although there is crime, there is scarcely a trace of violence. Instead just brilliant characterisation and a deep understanding of human nature.

'It demonstrates once again what I always knew – that the late Georges Simenon was one of the great writers of this century. It also demonstrates what I did not know – that Michael Gambon is a quite superb actor.'

Sadly, the only verdict that can now never be passed on this latest incarnation of Maigret is that of his creator, Georges Simenon. Comparisons are often invidious, but Michael Gambon has already done a great deal to show himself at least the equal of the best of his predecessors. And he promises to keep the magic of Maigret alive and flourishing for a while longer yet . . .

5:

THE MAIGRET FILMS

THIS IS A CHRONOLOGICAL listing of the films and television series about Chief Inspector Jules Maigret. They are listed under the name of the individual actors to play *le patron* with the titles, production companies and dates of release/transmission, plus producers, directors, scriptwriters, and the leading co-stars.

1. PIERRE RENOIR
La Nuit du Carrefour (The Crossroad Murders) SGPCF, 1932.
Produced by Jacques Becker. Directed by Jean Renoir.
Screenplay by Jean Renoir & Georges Simenon.
With: Marcel Forberge, Marie Stuart.

2. ABEL TARRIDE
Le Chien Jaune (A Face For a Clue), Tarride, 1932.
Produced & Directed by Jean Tarride.
Screenplay by Jean Tarride & Georges Simenon.
With: Albert Picard, Arlette Mery.

3. HARRY BAUR
La Tête d'un Homme (A Battle of Nerves) SGPCF, 1933.
Produced & Directed by Julian Duvivier.
Screenplay by Louis Delapree & Pierre Calman.
With: Alexandre Rignault, Gaston Jacquet, Marcel Bourdel, Gina Manes.

4. ALBERT PREJEAN
Picpus (To Any Lengths) SGPCF, 1943.
Produced & Directed by Roland Pottier.
Screenplay by Rene May.
With: Henri Echourin, Michel Vadet.
Cecile Est Morte (Maigret and the Spinster) SGPCF, 1943.
Produced & Directed by Maurice Tournier.
Screenplay by Rene May.
With: Michel Vadet, Lino Noro.
Les Caves du Majestic (Maigret at the Hotel Majestic)
SGPCF, 1945.
Produced & Directed by Roland Pottier.
Screenplay by Gilbert de Knyff.
With: Marcel Damia, Marthe Bessi.

5. CHARLES LAUGHTON
The Man on the Eiffel Tower. RKO Radio, 1949.
Produced & Directed by Irving Allen. (Additional scenes by
Charles Laughton)
Screenplay by Harry Brown & John Cortez.
With: Burgess Meredith, Robert Hutton, Franchot Tone,
Jean Wallace.

6.HERBERT BERGHOF
Stan the Killer. 'The Trap' CBS TV, 20 May 1950.
Directed by Joseph DeSantis.
Screenplay by David Gilman.
With: E. C. Marshall, Mary Powell.

7. ELI WALLACH
Stan the Killer. 'Studio One', CBS TV, 20 September 1952.
Directed by Paul Nickell.
Screenplay by Paul Monash.
With: Romney Brent, Lisa Ferraday.

8. MICHEL SIMON
Le Témoignage de l'Enfant de Choeur (Elusive Witness)
Terra Films, 1952.
Directed by Henry Verneuil.
Screenplay by J. Companeez & Henry Verneuil.
With: Claire Ollivier, Christian Fourcade, Jerome Goulven.
Le Bateau d'Emile. Calamy Films, 1962.
Directed by Denys de La Patelliere.
Screenplay by Andre Tabet.
With: Pierre Brasseur, Annie Giradot.

9. MAURICE MANSON
Maigret Mene l'Enquête. Films Francais, 1955.
Produced & Directed by Stany Cordier.
Screenplay by Rene May & Stany Cordier.
With: Albert Teynac, Rene Genin.

10. JEAN GABIN
Maigret Tend un Piège (Inspector Maigret) CFA, 1957.
Directed by Jean Delannoy.
Screenplay by Pierre Marcel & Jean Delannoy.
With Olivier Hussenot, Annie Giradot.
Maigret et l'Affaire Saint-Fiacre (*Maigret Keeps a Rendezvous*) CFA, 1959.
Directed by Jean Delannoy.

Screenplay by Jean Delannoy & Alan Jouvet.
With: Michel Auclair, Valentine Tessier.
Maigret Voit Rouge (Maigret Sees Red) CFA, 1963.
Directed by Gillies Grangier.
Screenplay: Claude Morgan.
With: Françoise Fabian, Vittorio Sanipoli.

11. BASIL SYDNEY

Maigret and the Lost Life. BBC TV, 4 December 1959.
Produced & Directed by Campbell Logan.
Screenplay by Giles Cooper.
With: Philip Guard (Lucas), Andre Van Gyseghem (Janvier),
Henry Oscar (Lognon), Anne Blake (Mme Maigret), Patrick
Troughton (Albert).

12. RUPERT DAVIES

Maigret, BBC TV 1960-1963.
Regular co-stars: Ewen Solan (Lucas), Helen Shingler (Madame
Maigret), Neville Jason (Lapointe), Victor Lucas (Torrence).
First Season (Executive Producer: Andrew Osborn)
1. *Murder in Montmarte*. 31 October 1960.
Directed by Andrew Osborn.
Screenplay by Giles Cooper.
With: Freda Jackson, April Olrich, Aubrey Woods, Thomas
Gallagher.
2. *Unscheduled Departure*. 7 November 1960.
Directed by Eric Taylor.
Screenplay by Giles Cooper.
With: Pamela Brown, Peter Copley, Charmian Eyre.
3. *The Burglar's Wife*. 14 November 1960.
Directed by Julian Amyes.
Screenplay by Roger East.
With: Hugh Burden, Noel Hood, Andree Melly.
4. *The Revolver*. 21 November 1960.
Directed by Chloe Gibson.
Screenplay by Roger East.
With: Margaretta Scott, Harold Scott, Dandy Nichols, Campbell
Singer.
5. *The Old Lady*. 28 November 1960.
Directed by Eric Taylor.
Screenplay by Margot Bennett.
With: Marie Ney, Neil McCarthy, Anthony Newlands.
6. *Liberty Bar*. 5 December 1960.
Directed by Andrew Osborn.

Screenplay by Margot Bennett.
With: Renee Houston, Paul Eddington, Colin Douglas, Erik Chitty.
7. *A Man of Quality*. 12 December 1960.
Directed by Gerard Glaister.
Screenplay by Giles Cooper.
With: Maurice Denham, Jean Anderson, Peter Barkworth, Charles Lloyd Pack, Wilfred Brambell.
8. *My Friend The Inspector*. 19 December 1960.
Directed by Eric Taylor.
Screenplay by Margot Bennett.
With: Marian Spencer, Pete Murray, Toke Townley, Leslie French.
9. *The Mistake*. 26 December 1960.
Directed by Andrew Osborn.
Screenplay by Roger East.
With: John Robinson, Annabel Maule, Peggy Thorpe-Bates, Valerie White, Eric Thompson.
10. *On Holiday*. 2 January 1961.
Directed by Eric Taylor.
Screenplay by Margot Bennett.
With: Griffiths Jones, Perlita Neilson, Bernard Kay, Nanette Newman.
11. *The Experts*. 9 January 1961.
Directed by Andrew Osborn.
Screenplay by Giles Cooper from the novel *Maigret, Lognon et les Gangsters*.
With: Henry Oscar, Bruno Barnabe, Sylva Langova, Lee Hamilton.
12. *The Cactus*. 16 January 1961.
Directed by Eric Taylor.
Screenplay by Roger East from the novel *Maigret Takes A Room*.
With: Sheila Burrell, Betty Baskcomb, Stratford Johns, Penny Morrell.
13. *The Children's Party*. 23 January 1961.
Directed by Gerard Glaister.
Screenplay by Giles Cooper from the novel *The Crime of Inspector Maigret*.
With: Alan Tilvern, George Little, Denis Holmes.

Second Season (Executive Producer: Andrew Osborn)
14. *Shadow Play*. 23 October 1961.
Directed by John Harrison.
Screenplay by Giles Cooper from the novel *Shadow on the Courtyard*.

With: Michael Barrington, Delena Kidd, Richard Martin.

15. *The Simple Case*. 30 October 1961.
Directed by Gerard Glaister.
Screenplay by Roger East from the novel, *Maigret at le Corps Sans Tête*.
With: Faith Brook, George Baker, Noel Howlett.

16. *Death of a Butcher*. 6 November 1961.
Directed by Andrew Osborn.
Screenplay by Giles Cooper from the novel *Un Echec de Maigret*.
With: Eric Pohlmann, Anthony Jacobs, Gwen Cherrell, Pauline Letts.

17. *The Winning Ticket*. 13 November 1961.
Directed by Harold Clayton.
Screenplay by Giles Cooper from the novel, *Maigret et Son Mort*.
With: George Pravda, Nadja Regin, Michael Reeves, Michael Ripper, Marianne Stone.

18. *Inspector Lognon's Triumph*. 20 November 1961.
Directed by John Harrison.
Screenplay by Giles Cooper from the novel, *Maigret et l'Inspecteur Malgracieux*.
With: Henry Oscar, Delphi Lawrence, Ann Firbank, Leslie Glazer, Warren Mitchell.

19. *The Lost Sailor*. 27 November 1961
Directed by Gerard Glaister.
Screenplay by Margot Bennett from the novel, *Port des Brumes*.
With: Frederick Schiller, Alan Wheatley, John Forbes-Robertson, Iris Russell.

20. *The Golden Fleece*. 4 December 1961.
Directed by Rudolph Cartier.
Screenplay by Giles Cooper from the novel, *L'Ecluse No.1*.
With: Francis de Wolfe, Michael Brennan, Jan Kenny, Al Mulock.

21. *Raise Your Right Hand*. 11 December 1961.
Directed by Andrew Osborn.
Screenplay by Roger East from the novel *Maigret aux Assises*.
With: Gene Anderson, Patrick Troughton, Edward Evans.

22. *The Liars* 18 December 1961.
Directed by Rudolph Cartier.
Screenplay by Vincent Tilsley from the novel *Maigret à l'Ecole*.
With: Joseph Furst, Rita Webb, Patrick Newell, Victor Platt.

23. *A Crime for Christmas*. 26 December 1961.
Directed by Campbell Logan.
Screenplay by Margot Bennett from the novel *Un Noël de Maigret*.

With: Barry Foster, Heather Chasen, Esma Cannon, Jenny
Laird, George Coulouris, Toke Townley.
24. *The Reluctant Witnesses*. 1 January 1962.
Directed by Gerard Glaister.
Screenplay by Donald Bull from the novel *Maigret et les Temoints
Récalcitrants*.
With: Jean Cadell, Peter Sallis, Althea Parker, John
Hawksworth.
25. *The White Hat*. 8 January 1962.
Directed by Gerard Glaister.
Screenplay by Roger East from the novel, *L'Amie de Madame
Maigret*.
With: John Carson, Edwin Richfield, Frank Shelley, Edith
Saville.
26. *Murder on Monday*. 15 January 1962.
Directed by Terence Williams.
Screenplay by Giles Cooper from the novel *Maigret et l'Homme
du Banc*.
With: Sylvia Kay, Madge Ryan, Jack Rodney, Stratford Johns,
Tom Adams.

Third Season (Executive Producer: Andrew Osborn)
27. *Voices From The Past*. 24 September 1962.
Directed by Gerard Glaister.
Screenplay by Giles Cooper from the novel *Maigret et les Vieillards*.
With: Terence Alexander, Fay Compton, Charles Gray,
Catherine Lacey, Richard Vernon.
28. *The Madman of Vervac*. 1 October 1962.
Directed by Andrew Osborn.
Screenplay by Roger East from the novel *Le Fou de Bergerac*.
With: Laurence Payne, Pauline Yates, Roger Delgardo,
Lockwood West.
29. *The Countess*. 8 October 1962.
Directed by Andrew Osborn.
Screenplay by Roger East from the novel *L'Affaire Saint-Fiacre*.
With: William Franklyn, Clive Morton, William Mervyn, Philip
Stone, Colin Jeavons.
30. *The Wedding Guest*. 15 October 1962.
Directed by Terence Williams.
Screenplay by Giles Cooper from the novel *La Guinguette à Deux
Sous*.
With: John Slater, Philip Lathan, Katherine Blake, Peter
Madden, Frank Williams.
31. *High Politics*. 22 October 1962.

Directed by Andrew Osborn.
Screenplay by Roger East from the novel *Maigret Chez le Ministre*.
With: Noel Johnston, Betty McDowall, Leonard Sachs, Ellen Pollock, William Devlin.
32. *Love from Felicie*. 29 October 1962.
Directed by Andrew Osborn.
Screenplay by Giles Cooper from the novel *Felicie Est Là*.
With: Lana Morris, Olaf Pooley, Anthony Morton, Alan Browning.
33. *The Dirty House*. 5 November 1962.
Directed by Terence Williams.
Screenplay by Giles Cooper from the novel *Maigret Se Fâche*.
With: Beatrix Lehmann, Nicolette Bernard, Rosalie Crutchley, Ernest Clark, Christopher Sandford.
34. *The Crystal Ball*. 12 November 1962.
Directed by John Harrison.
Screenplay by Roger East from the novel *Signe Picpus*.
With: Neal Arden, John Kidd, Robert Bernal, Linda Gardner.
35. *The Crooked Castle*. 19 November 1962.
Directed by Andrew Osborn.
Screenplay by Donald Bull from the novel, *La Nuit du Carrefour*.
With: Kevin Brennan, Gerard Heinz, Lisa Daniely, Roland Curram, Charles Farrell.
36. *Death in Mind*. 26 November 1962.
Directed by John Elliott.
Screenplay by Giles Cooper & John Elliott from the novel *La Tête d'un Homme*.
With: Anton Rodgers, John Ronane, Gabriella Licudi, Robin Chapman.
37. *Seven Little Crosses*. 3 December 1962.
Directed by Gerard Glaister.
Screenplay by Giles Cooper from the novel *Sept Petites Croix dans un Carnet*.
With: Alfred Burke, James Maxwell, Arthur Lowe, Fanny Carby.
38. *The Amateurs*. 17 December 1962.
Directed by Terence Williams.
Screenplay by Donald Bull from the novel *Le Voleur Paresseux*.
With: Mervyn Johns, Georgina Cookson, George Pastell, Trader Faulkner, Edwin Richfield, Alan Howard.

Fourth Series (Executive Producer: Andrew Osborn)
39. *Poor Cecile!* 1 October 1963.
Directed by Michael Hayes.

Screenplay by Donald Bull from the novel *Cecille Est Morte*.
With: Joan Sanderson, Anthony Jacobs, Mary Chester, Brian
Waldron.

40. *The Fontonay Murders*. 8 October 1963.
Directed by Alan Bridges.
Screenplay by Elaine Morgan from the novel *Maigret a Peur*.
With: Edward Chapman, Margaret Rawlings, Alan Wheatley,
Norman Scace, Alan Rowe.

41. *The Lost Life*. 15 October 1963.
Directed by Gilchrist Calder.
Screenplay by Giles Cooper from the novel *La Jeune Morte*.
With: Henry Oscar, Olga Lindo, Patsy Smart, Marne Maitland,
Vanda Godsell, Eileen Way.

42. *The Cellars of the Majestic*. 22 October 1963.
Directed by Eric Tayler.
Screenplay by Anthony Steven from the novel *Les Caves du
Majestic*.
With: Redmond Phillips, Peter Dyneley, Sheila Brennan, Ivor
Salter, George Coulouris.

43. *A Man Condemned*. 29 October 1968.
Directed by Terence Williams.
Screenplay by Roger East from the novel *Une Confidence de
Maigret*.
With: Patricia Laffan, Terence de Marnay, Ballard Berkeley,
Trader Faulkner, Philip Madoc.

44. *The Flemish Shop*. 5 November 1963.
Directed by Eric Tayler.
Screenplay by Rex Rucker from the novel *Chez les Flamands*.
With: Margaret Tyzack, Joyce Carey, Mike Leigh, Grace
Arnold, Michael Brennan.

45. *A Taste of Power*. 12 November 1963.
Directed by Terence Williams.
Screenplay by Donald Bull from the novel *La Premiere Enquete
de Maigret*.
With: John Carson, Terence Alexander, William Mendall,
Margaret Elliott.

46. *The Log of the Cap Fagnet*. 19 November 1963.
Directed by Michael Hayes.
Screenplay by Elaine Morgan from the novel *Au Rendezvous des
Terre-Neuvas*.
With: Victor Platt, Jerrold Wells, Thomas Baptiste, Alex Farrell,
John Hollis.

47. *The Judge's House*. 26 November 1963.
Directed by Terence Dudley.

Screenplay by Elaine Morgan from the novel *La Maison du Juge*.
With: Leslie French, Lyn Ashley, Raymond Mason, Patricia Hayes, Paul Bacon.
48. *Another World*. 3 December 1963.
Directed by Michael Hayes.
Screenplay by Donald Bull from the novel *Maigret Voyage*.
With: Clare Kelly, Alan MacNaughtan, Moira Redmond, Ferdy Mayne.
49. *The Crime at Lock 14*. 10 December 1963.
Directed by Andrew Osborn.
Screenplay by Anthony Coburn from the novel *Le Charretier de la Providence*.
With: Hugh Burden, Isa Miranda, Andrew Faulds. Paul Whitsun-Jones, Philip Ray.
50. *Peter the Lett*. 17 December 1963.
Directed by Rudolph Cartier.
Screenplay by Giles Cooper from the novel *Pietr le Letton*.
With: Marius Goring, Peter Illing, Arthur Ridley, Roger Delgardo, Magda Miller.
51. *Maigret's Little Joke*. 24 December 1963.
Directed by Terence Williams.
Screenplay by Donald Bull from the novel *Maigret S'amuse*.
With: Michael Goodliffe, Neil McCallum, Stephanie Bidmead, Shelagh Fraser, Barry Letts.

13. **GINO CERVI**
Inspector Maigret. RAI-TV 1962-1973.
Produced by Mario Attene.
Script Editor Giuseppe Pasquarelli.
With: Enzo Bertello, Luigi de Cesari.

14. **HEINZ RUHMANN**
Maigret. ARD 1965-1958.
Produced by Gunther Albrecht.
Script Editor Michael Stohl.
With: Manfred Niehaus, Walter Keil.

15. **JAN TEULING**
Inspector Maigret. OTP 1965.
Produced by Andries Overste.
Script Editor Louis Vermolt.
With: Fred Heinemen, Rudi Gelman.

16. JEAN RICHARD
Maigret. Antenne 2 1965-.
Produced by Jean-Pierre Mondant.
Script Editor Dominique Marne.
With: Paul Mantaigne, Jean Didier.

17. BORIS TENINE
Detective Maigret. Studio Lenfilm 1969.
Produced by Yevgeny Kanevski.
Script Editor Vladimir Schukina.
With: Pavel Nazarov, Vladimir Popova.

18. KINYA AIKAWA
Maigret. NTV 1970-.
Produced by Setsuko Mikuni.
Script Editor Yuki Ebara.
With: Choko Ida, Shinjiro Ebara.

19. RICHARD HARRIS
Maigret. HTV, 21 May 1988.
Produced by Arthur Weingarten.
Directed by Paul Lynch.
Screenplay by Arthur Weingarten.
With: Andrew McCulloch (Lucas), Barbara Shelley (Mme Maigret), Patrick O'Neal, Victoria Tennant, Ian Ogilvy, Don Henderson, Caroline Munro.

20. BRUNO CREMER
Maigret. Dune, 1991-.
Produced by Robert Nador, Eve Vercel and Steve Hawes.
Directors: Jose Pinehiro, Claude Goretta, Serge Leroy and Bertrand Van Effenterre.
Scriptwriters: Jacques Cortal, Serge Leroy, Santiago Amigorena.
With: Serge Beauvois (Torrence), Philippe Polet (Lapointe), Jean-Claude Frissung (Janvier), Alexis Nitzar (Lognon).

21. MICHAEL GAMBON
Maigret. Granada, 1992-.
Producer Jonathan Alwyn.
Directors John Glenister and James Cellan Jones.
Screenplays by Alan Plater, William Humble, Douglas Livingtone and Robin Chapman.
Regular co-stars: Geoffrey Hutchings (Sgt. Lucas), Jack

Galloway (Insp. Janvier), James Larking (Insp. Lapointe), Ciaran Madden (Mme Maigret). John Moffat (M. Comeliau), Christian Rodska (Moers).

First Season
1 *The Patience of Maigret*. 9 February 1992.
Directed by James Cellan Jones.
Screenplay by Alan Plater.
With: Cheryl Campbell, Trevor Peacock, Rachel Fielding, Greg Hicks, Ann Todd.
2. *Maigret and the Burglar's Wife*. 16 February 1992.
Directed by John Glenister.
Screenplay by Alan Plater.
With: Sandy Ratcliff, Margery Withers, Christopher Benjamin, Melinda Kendall, Vilma Hollingbery.
3. *Maigret Goes To School*. 23 February 1992.
Directed by James Cellan Jones.
Screenplay by William Humble.
With: Adrian Lukis, Struan Rodger, Joanna David, Max Beazley, Godfrey James.
4. *Maigret and the Mad Woman*. 2 March 1992.
Directed by John Glenister.
Screenplay by William Humble.
With: Marjorie Sommerville, Mark Lockyer, Mark Frankel, Frances Cuka, Harold Innocent.
5. *Maigret on Home Ground*. 9 March 1992.
Directed by James Cellan Jones.
Screenplay by Robin Chapman.
With: Daniel Moynihan, Jonathan Adams, James Clyde, John Warnaby, Gareth Thomas, Paul Brightwell.
6. *Maigret Sets A Trap*. 16 March 1992.
Directed by John Glenister.
Screenplay by Douglas Livingstone.
With: Ann Mitchell, Richard Willis, Leonie Mellinger, Catherine Russell, Jonathan Tafler.

Second Season
Producer Paul Marcus.
Directors John Strickland, Stuart Burge and Nick Renton.
Screenplays by William Humble, Douglas Livingstone and Bill Gallagher.
Regular co-stars: Geoffrey Hutchings (Sgt. Lucas), Jack Galloway (Insp. Janvier), James Larkin (Insp. Laporte), Barbara Flynn (Mme. Maigret).

7. *Maigret and the Night Club Dancer*. 14 March 1993.
Directed by John Strickland.
Screenplay by Douglas Livingstone.
With: Minnie Driver, Sandor Korospatsky, Tony Doyle, Brenda
Blethyn, Jill Freud, Michael Billington.

8. *Maigret and The Hotel Majestic*. 21 March 1993.
Directed by Nick Renton.
Screenplay by William Rumble.
With: Michael J. Jackson, Nicola Duffet, Clifford Rose, John
Kavanagh, Toyah Willcox, Roger Hume.

9. *Maigret on the Defensive*. 28 March 1993.
Directed by Stuart Burge.
Screenplay by William Humble.
With: Pip Torrens, Deborah Findlay, Oliver Ford Davies, John
Benfield, Liza Walker, John Salthouse.

10. *Maigret's Boyhood Friend*. 4 April 1993.
Directed by John Strickland.
Screenplay by William Humble.
With: Edward Petherbridge, Betty Marsden, Alan David, Peter
Blythe, Kenneth Haigh.

11. *Maigret and the Minister*. 11 April 1993.
Directed by Nick Renton.
Screenplay by Bill Gallagher.
With: Peter Barkworth, Eileen Page, Michael Melia, Jane
Wymark, Sorcha Cusak, John Hartley.

12. *Maigret and the Maid*. 18 April 1993.
Directed by Stuart Burge.
Screenplay by Douglas Livingstone.
With: Edward Tudor Pole, Ralph Nossek, Susie Lindeman,
Christopher Ryan, Tony Rohr, Paul Moriarty.

INDEX

(Figures in **bold** refer to illustrations)